THE STORY OF WORLD WAR II

Landmark
Giant

Illustrated with photographs & maps

THE STORY OF

WORLD WAR II

BY ROBERT LECKIE

RANDOM HOUSE ▪ NEW YORK

Grateful acknowledgment is made to Doubleday & Company, Inc. for permission to use on pages 99 and
142 quotations from *Crusade in Europe* by Dwight D. Eisenhower. Copyright, 1948, by Doubleday &
Company, Inc.

PHOTOGRAPH CREDITS: British Information Services, page 48; Cecil Beaton, 50 (bottom); Defense Department /U.S. Marine Corps, 121, 122, 124, 125, 127, 128, 130, 133, 164, 177, 180, 181; European Picture Service, 65 (bottom); Imperial War Museum, 31 (top), 33 (right), 35, 51, 54 (right), 60, 63, 93 (bottom), 94,
139, 157; National Archives /U.S. Navy, 71, 85, 144 (top), 168; Pix, 50 (top), 93 (top), 105; Sovfoto, 66,
104, 161; Underwood & Underwood, 46; United Press International, 15, 16, 18, 20, 29, 31 (bottom), 33
(left), 47, 55, 56, 62, 65 (top), 79, 86 (bottom), 89, 90 (top), 102, 147 (bottom), 148, 153, 155, 162, 169, 171;
United Seamen's Service, 101; U.S. Air Force, 116, 118, 135, 136, 159; U.S. Army, 61, 67, 75, 76, 90 (bot-
tom), 98, 108, 109, 111, 141, 151, 152, 165, 172, 175, 185; U.S. Navy, 86 (top); Wide World, 12, 13, 22, 24,
26, 38, 39, 41, 43, 44, 52, 54 (left), 57, 72, 74, 82, 97, 110, 138, 144 (bottom), 147 (top), 149, 174, 179.
HALF TITLE & TITLE PAGES: Defense Department /U.S. Marine Corps.
ENDPAPER: Top—U.S. Air Force; Bottom (left to right)—U.S. Army, Defense Department /U.S. Marine
Corps, Defense Department /U.S. Marine Corps; Imperial War Museum; Defense Department /U.S.
Marine Corps.
COVER: The picture which appears on the jacket and cover of the book was supplied through the cour-
tesy of the Twentieth Century-Fox Film Corporation.

TO THE BALL ROAD BOYS—

*Andy, Artie, Danny, Dougie,
Chris, Geoff, Kevin, and Johnny*

Contents

THE STORY OF WORLD WAR II

The War Begins | 1

The greatest war in history began at dawn of September 1, 1939.

On that day Germany invaded neighboring Poland, attacking without warning and with such shattering power and speed that the world gasped to see how easily the first step in Adolf Hitler's plan for world conquest was being carried out.

England and France declared war on Germany two days after the invasion, but it was already clear that the unprepared Allies would never be able to come to Poland's side in time. The Germans had introduced something new in the history of warfare—the *blitzkrieg*, or lightning war. The blitzkrieg was based on two key weapons—the tank and the airplane—hurled suddenly and in great numbers on an unsuspecting foe.

First the German *Luftwaffe*, or air force, destroyed the Polish air force. Using approximately 1,400 airplanes—to about 450 for the Poles—the Luftwaffe spent the first day making surprise attacks at the Polish airfields. They caught most of the Polish airplanes on the ground and shot them to pieces. The next day they finished the job. The Polish air force had been annihilated in two days with scarcely as much as a single air battle.

Once this had been accomplished, the German tanks or *Panzer* units were free to roll without fear of air attack.

And roll they did. The tanks led the two massive German armies which plunged into Poland from north and south. They clanked deep into the Polish rear, striking for the enemy army's nerve centers: road and railway junctions, bridges, tunnels, telegraph stations, and airfields. Polish infantrymen were powerless to stop them. Their bullets rattled harmlessly off the tanks' thick steel hides, while the men themselves had only their shirts to protect them against the cannon shells and machine-gun bullets of the tanks.

The Polish cavalry was also helpless. In charge after hopeless charge, horses and men went down in a kicking, useless slaughter which marked the end of the era of mounted warriors. The German tanks roared on, seizing every road, splitting off into column after column in a literal swarming of metal monsters. They made it impossible for the Poles to form a solid battle front.

After the tanks came the armored cars, the motorcycle troops, and finally the foot soldiers, or infantry, supported by horse-drawn artillery. These last were the formations which applied the knockout blow, steadily mopping up pocket after pocket of Polish infantry whom the mechanized forces had chopped up piecemeal and left behind them.

Meanwhile, the Luftwaffe was completing the destruction of the Polish army's communications and road nets.

11

Swarming into a Polish village, a column of motorized German soldiers fans out in two directions.

They bombed bridges, road centers, railroad stations, and radio stations. They struck at all the Polish troop concentrations. The Polish rear was paralyzed. It was not possible for the Polish front-line troops to make orderly withdrawals. It was also impossible to get reinforcements up to them.

The havoc and confusion were further complicated when the Germans deliberately unleashed a calculated terror upon the civilian population. Clouds of dreaded *Stuka* dive bombers fell on defenseless cities. They drove terrified civilians out into the roads, turning these vital highways into one impassable mass of wrecked vehicles and struggling human misery. The Stukas even had ear-splitting whistles installed

in their wings to magnify the terror of their dives.

And so the German blitz blasted everything before it. The Polish cities and centers of opposition fell one by one to the arrogant and exultant invaders in steel helmets. To the west, Poland's allies were unable to come to her side. Once again the democracies were unprepared for war. England had only a few divisions of men to spare, and by October would have only four of them on the European continent. France had more than a hundred divisions mobilized—she was thought to possess the most powerful army in Europe—but they were not nearly so well equipped as the Germans. All that France could do to help Poland was to send a series of strong patrols into Germany's western frontiers. Meeting stiff opposition, the French pulled back behind their own defensive position, known as the Maginot Line.

Poland, meanwhile, was contributing to her own swift downfall. Outnumbered twenty to one in tanks and two to one in fire power, the Poles still had about 600,000 men to oppose the million-man German invasion force. Had Poland used these forces skillfully, she might still have won precious time in which her allies could have armed and come to her rescue. And if the Polish army had pulled back to a good fighting position roughly in the middle of the country, and inside a number of river barriers, she might still have held off the Germans.

But Poland tried to defend everywhere along her long western border—

from the Baltic Sea in the north to the Carpathian Mountains in the south. Her forces were spread thin, and the freewheeling Panzer divisions tore them to bits.

Then, on September 17, came the stab in the back. Russia invaded Poland. In accordance with a secret agreement defining spheres of influence, which Russian Premier Joseph Stalin had made with Hitler in August, Poland's eastern neighbor rushed in for her share of the spoils.

Caught between two fires, Poland was forced to face the fact that it was now only a matter of time. The Polish troops made their last gallant stand in the capital city of Warsaw. Here the Poles fought on with the stubborn bravery for which they are famous. But on September 27 Warsaw finally fell. It was all over. The next day foreign ministers Joachim von Ribbentrop of Germany and Vyacheslav Molotov of Russia met to divide prostrate Poland.

Almost half of Poland's 150,000 square miles—including most of her mines and factories—were taken over by Germany. And at least twenty-two

A squadron of Stuka dive bombers.

million of her thirty-five million people were placed under German "protecttion." Russia took the rest, along with Poland's oil resources.

Hitler's eastern flank had been secured by the lightning Polish conquest, as well as by his new-found friendship with Stalin. Now the German leader was free to turn toward the west.

German troops occupy the Polish city of Warsaw.

2 | Why the War Began

It all seemed to have happened before, although not with such stunning speed.

Twenty-five years earlier, in August of 1914, the Germany of Kaiser Wilhelm had engulfed the world in the flames of the global conflict known as World War I. Out of that First World War had come the seeds of the second. Many historians feel these seeds were sown by the severe terms which the victorious Allies imposed on Germany through the Treaty of Versailles.

Whether or not the terms were truly harsh, the Allies—especially France— were determined to crush forever the Prussian military spirit that had guided Germany. Prussia was the militaristic north German state which had organized and led the new German Empire. Prussian militarism had caused three invasions of France in a hundred years, and the "blood-and-iron" Prussian spirit was blamed for the five dreadful years of World War I.

There had never before been such a war. Measured in human lives alone, the casualties included thirteen million dead soldiers, thirteen million dead civilians, twenty million wounded soldiers, three million prisoners, nine million war orphans, five million war widows, and ten million refugees. The dead numbered twice as many as all those who had perished in all the major wars fought between 1790 and 1913. To this hideous loss of life must be added

the enormous costs of waging war—at one time there were sixty-five million men under arms—as well as frightful destruction of property. The total bill has been estimated at three hundred and thirty-one billion, six hundred million dollars!

Twenty years after the start of the war, the magazine *Scholastic* estimated that the cost of World War I would have provided:

1. Every family in England, France, Belgium, Germany, Russia, the United States, Canada, and Australia with a $2,500 house on a $500 one-acre lot, with $1,000 worth of furniture; and

2. A $5,000,000 library for every community of 200,000 population in each of the countries; and

3. A $10,000,000 university for each of these communities; and

4. A fund that at 5 per cent interest would yield enough to pay indefinitely $1,000 a year to 125,000 teachers and 125,000 nurses, and

5. Still leave enough funds to purchase every piece of property and all the wealth in Belgium and France at a fair market price.

So the Allies, who had suffered two-thirds of the casualties and the costs, were naturally determined to prevent another such war. To do this, they

German soldiers march through one of the countless French villages completely demolished by World War I.

created "buffers" all around Germany's borders. The country of Poland, which had passed out of existence in 1795, was brought back into being and enlarged by land from Germany. The Austro-Hungarian Empire, Germany's chief ally, was broken up. A tiny and weak Austria was left on Germany's south, with the new state of Czechoslovakia on the southeast. And on the west, all of the German land west of the Rhine River was held by the Allies.

All of Germany's overseas empire was given to the new League of Nations. This League was to be the world peace-keeping body, similar in concept to our present-day United Nations. Then Germany's former overseas possessions were divided among Allied states, which were to run them as "mandates" for the League. Japan, one of the Allies in World War I, received many of these German territories in the Pacific Ocean, although she had done almost no fighting. Here was another seed of World War II: Japan used her island mandates to build her own military power.

The Treaty of Versailles also limited the German army to 100,000 men, just enough to police the country, and the German navy was reduced to 15,000. An air force was forbidden.

One of the severest blows of all to the defeated German nation was the bill of thirty-three billion dollars in war damages presented by the Allies. The initial installments of this bill were to be paid in commodities which the new German Republic said were needed for German recovery. The new government was a shaky one. The country had passed through a revolution at the end of the First World War. Although it did not become communistic as had its Russian neighbor, it still had to contend with an active Communist party.

Although the Germans protested bitterly against the Treaty, the Allies insisted that it be accepted in full. Germany had no choice. A wave of anger soon swept over the country, and Matthias Erzberger, who had advised Germany to sign the treaty, was murdered.

As the decade of the Twenties opened, Germany complained more

15

and more of her inability to pay the war-damage bill. When it became clear that she was not going to pay, France marched into the Ruhr, the industrial heart of Germany. This happened in January, 1923, and it had the effect of bringing chaos to Germany. Inflation set in. The same amount of money bought less and less. By late 1923 German money was not worth the paper it was printed on. Workers carried their salaries home in wheelbarrows. To mail a letter to the United States cost a billion marks. Just one American dollar was worth a mountain of marks measurable in thirteen figures. (In 1964, by contrast, an American dollar was worth four German marks.)

Unemployment, hunger, and hardship stalked the land.

The Allies were shocked. They also feared that such chaos would provide just the climate in which Communism might flourish. So the war-damage bill was softened; the French left the Ruhr, and loans were made to the German government. The United States made most of these loans. From about 1924 to 1929, Germany recovered and prospered. Then came 1929, the year of the Great Depression. It started in America and spread rapidly throughout the world. It struck industrial countries such as Germany the hardest. There was another German economic crash. And this set the stage for the entry of that strange, pale and malevolent leader whose name was Adolf Hitler.

Suffering from the privations of the depression, German civilians stand in line to exchange their possessions for food.

The son of a minor customs official, Hitler was born in Austria on April 20, 1889. While still a young man he went to the capital city of Vienna, and there he came to hate the Jews and other "inferior races," as he called them, who lived in this cosmopolitan city. He dreamed of a world led by "pure" Aryans or Germans: tall, strong, blond, and handsome. Hitler himself was short, pasty-faced, and dumpy—although he had the wild burning eyes of a fanatic.

At the age of twenty-four Hitler left Vienna for Munich, Germany. There he found happiness. He liked the people of Bavaria, the German state of which Munich is the capital. They were his pure Germans. When World War I broke out, Hitler joined a Bavarian regiment and fought with distinction, rising to the rank of corporal. Coming out of the army after the war, he saw his beloved Germany in ruins. Immediately he blamed the disaster on the Jews and traitors.

Returning to Munich, Hitler took over what was to be the National Socialist Party, (*Nationalsozialistische*) called "Nazi" from its initials. He tried to gain control of the Bavarian state government by force, but his revolt failed and Hitler was jailed. In his cell, he wrote the major portion of a book, *Mein Kampf* (My Struggle), outlining exactly how he expected to conquer the world. Had more Allied statesmen read this book after Hitler came to power in Germany, they might well have prevented the calamity of World War II. But at the time few people outside Germany took it seriously.

After Hitler got out of prison, he returned to his Nazi followers. He drew around him the little band of ruthless lieutenants who were to become world-famous. There was Hermann Goering, an aviation hero of the First World War who would become a fat, swashbuckling figure fond of wearing gaudy uniforms and carrying a diamond-studded baton. Goering would build and command the Luftwaffe, the German air force. The Nazi minister of propaganda was Dr. Joseph Goebbels, a dwarfish man with a club foot and piercing eyes that stared out of an oversized head. Goebbels had failed as a writer, but he would fill the periodicals of the world with all of his frenzied lies about the Jews and the "betrayal" of Versailles. Herr Heinrich Himmler was another of these devoted followers who called Hitler *Der Führer,* or the leader. This neat little sparrow of a man—mediocre and modest in his rimless glasses and pressed plain suits—was to turn into one of the cruellest murderers in history. As head of the German police, including the infamous *Gestapo* or secret state police, Himmler was responsible for sending millions to torture and death.

17

Adolf Hitler (sitting, right) poses with a group of comrades in the 16th Bavarian Reserve Infantry Regiment.

Backed by such men, Hitler gradually extended his influence in Germany. He was now trying to gain power by political means, to gain by guile or treachery what he could not take by force. Hitler had learned his lesson in Bavaria, and he would never again use violence until all the big battalions were on his side.

The Nazis began running for office in the German parliament. In good times they did not do so well; in bad times they were successful. Like the Communists, the Nazis needed unhappy people who would listen to them blaming every misfortune on traitors or other scapegoats. The inflation of the early Twenties had wiped out the savings of the middle-class people and left them destitute. They were unhappy and

On the window of a Jewish store a Nazi storm trooper posts a sign—"Germans! Watch out! Don't buy from Jews!"

uprooted and ready to follow the lead of an adventurer such as Hitler, who promised to end unemployment and provide them with all sorts of luxuries if they would just join him.

There was also another group of Germans who flocked to Hitler's standard of the crooked black cross or *Swastika*. These others were called the Free Corps. Most of them were former soldiers. They had no trades or skills. They mourned all the lost glories of Kaiser Wilhelm's Germany. Heroes during the war, they were now nobodies. They resented this position, and they hated the Treaty of Versailles as a "slave" treaty. From this Free Corps Hitler was able to recruit many of the Storm Troopers who made up his private army.

By the end of 1932 Hitler had reached a new height in political power. By that time, also, the government of Germany, under the impact of the Great Depression which was eating away the structure of society, had turned to what one historian has called "naked gangsterism." In most of the big cities the nights were made hideous by the Nazis and the Communists fighting each other in the streets. There were frequent strikes.

As 1933 began, there was a government crisis. The Nazi party did not control enough votes in the parliament to make Hitler the German chancellor. But they had enough strength to make it impossible for any other party to rule without their help. So Hitler refused to assist any other party unless he was made chancellor. His cause was helped by the fact that the leaders of the other big parties hated and distrusted each other. Moreover, the president of Germany, the venerable General Paul von Hindenburg, hero of World War I, was now a senile old man. And it was he who had the power of offering the chancellorship. He forgot his old contempt for Hitler as "the little corporal" whom he would put to work "licking stamps with my picture on them." On January 30, 1933, he gave the chancellorship to Adolf Hitler—and the lights began going out all over Germany.

Six months after he became chancellor, Adolf Hitler was the undisputed dictator of Germany. He bullied parliament and strangled the Republic with a rope of Nazi laws. He crushed all opposition. Anyone who challenged him directly was packed off to a concentration camp. Within the ranks of his own party, Hitler put down a "revolt"—real or imagined—which left him completely in charge. On June 30, 1934, Hitler executed Ernest Roehm, the man who had built the Storm Troops. Thousands of others were also killed in a dreadful bloodbath called "The Night of the Long Knives."

This was done not only to get rid of Roehm and other "unreliables." It also assured the leaders of the German army that they would no longer have to deal with a second army—the Storm Troops —in Germany. Hitler needed the Prussian generals. They would build the army that he planned to turn loose in Europe. After President von Hindenburg died, Hitler made the German of-

ficers swear personal vows of loyalty to him.

The Fuehrer also needed German industry to supply his *Wehrmacht,* or armed forces. So he befriended businessmen and industrialists. Many Germans thought Adolf Hitler was the savior of their country. He started things moving again in Germany, and his personal magnetism charmed many important persons who should have been wiser.

But when Hitler turned to the persecution of religion he showed his true colors. Although he did his worst when he unleashed his fury on the Jews, he also attacked the Protestant and Catholic Churches. Christianity preaches faith in a Supreme God and the brotherhood of all men as equal before God. But Hitler wanted faith in no one but himself, the Fuehrer, and he preached the gospel of a master race of Germans with contempt for all others.

In the end, Hitler's campaign against Christianity failed. And with the coming of the war, the anti-Christian persecution died down. But the steady persecution of the Jewish people did not subside. It began unofficially in 1933; then in 1935 it became official. In that year a law was passed stripping Jews of all their rights. They were less than slaves. Anyone who had a grievance might take it out on a Jew without fear of punishment. Armed with this law, Herr Himmler set his vast police force to work on "the final settlement of the Jewish question."

To the Nazis being a Jew was a crime. Thus, following a conference in

1941 where the "final settlement" was formalized, Himmler and his men systematically set about the robbery, torture and death of an entire race. Subjected to every indignity, driven from their homes, stripped naked, spat upon, forced to clean streets with their tongues, robbed of all that they owned, the Jews were herded off to concentration camps to meet the inevitable end of hunger, degradation and indecent death. In all, six million European Jews died.

Thus did Adolf Hitler unleash the Nazi bestiality in his own country. And by 1935 he was ready to export it. As Dr. Goebbels said in one of his numerous slogans: "Germany today, and tomorrow the world!"

Hitler, Hermann Goering (center), and Joseph Goebbels (right) salute during the singing of the national song.

Hitler's Partners | 4

Adolf Hitler was to have two partners in his venture into world conquest.

The first was the Italian dictator, Benito Mussolini. Short, but with a commanding shaved head which gave the impression of great strength, Mussolini had also come to power in a time of crisis. In 1922 all of Italy was in upheaval. In that year, Mussolini's Fascist party made their famous march on Rome. He put down the rival Communists and took over the government. He also took a title: *Il Duce,* or the leader.

Thereafter the short figure of Il Duce shouting from his Roman balcony became a familiar sight in the world's newspapers. To his credit, Mussolini tried to help his country. Industry and agriculture were improved. Unemployment was ended by the simple trick of putting the jobless in the army. Roads were built. And Il Duce's greatest boast was that he made the sloppy Italian railroads run on time. Many clear-sighted men admired Mussolini, among them Winston Churchill.

Hitler's other partner was to be the island empire of Japan. Japan had a military dictatorship. Generals and admirals ran the country. They were in league with the rich factory owners, and they controlled the people through the Emperor Hirohito. In Japan, the emperor was believed to be divine. Hirohito's word was law. But he seldom gave orders. The military men gave them. They had only to say, "The Emperor wills it," and it was done.

These militarists in Japan had been in control since the end of the previous century. In 1904-05 Japan had astounded the world by destroying the Russian navy and defeating the Russian army. Then after World War I, Japan was given many of defeated Germany's islands in the Pacific. She fortified these outposts against the orders of the League of Nations. By the end of the Twenties, Japan had also built one of the mightiest navies afloat and was enlarging her army.

As the Thirties began, this was the world picture:

The nations of Germany, Italy, and Japan had been organized by iron and brutal rule and had rearmed themselves. The free democracies—England, France, the United States—had disarmed themselves. Worse, the Great Depression had caused havoc in these democracies. The League of Nations, which was to keep the peace, had been crippled by America's refusal to join it, while America herself had withdrawn from world affairs. Finally, Germany, Italy, and Japan were dissatisfied. They complained that they had been deprived of their fair share of the earth's surface and riches. They said the democracies were "have" nations and they were "have-nots."

Japan was the first to move.

The Italian dictator, Benito Mussolini, strikes a familiar pose as he addresses the public from a balcony.

In 1931, she invaded China and began the campaign by which she eventually seized the vast province of Manchuria.

Mussolini acted next.

In 1935 his troops attacked little Ethiopia on the east coast of Africa. Il Duce shouted that he was going to create a new Roman Empire.

In both cases the League of Nations did little. Although the democracies protested loudly, they gave no real assistance to either China or Ethiopia.

Impressed by the easy success of Japan and Italy, Hitler began to make his own demands.

First, in 1935, he got back part of his western lands known as the Saar. The next year he put troops and guns back into the Rhineland on the west. This was forbidden by the Treaty of Ver-

sailles. But Hitler scornfully called the treaty "a mere scrap of paper." Once again the democracies closed their eyes.

In that same year, 1936, both Hitler and Mussolini had a chance to train their armies and air forces in a real war. This was the terrible and bloody Spanish Civil War which began when a number of generals in the Spanish army revolted against the government. They were led by General Francisco Franco, and they won the war. Hitler and Il Duce sent military help to Franco, and tried out such new war horrors as the mass bombing of helpless cities. The loyalist government side was helped by Russia, and the Communists eventually took over the entire losing cause.

While this war was going on, Hitler and Mussolini drew closer and closer until the alliance known as The Axis was formed between them. Japan, still busy in China, would join later.

In 1938 Hitler began moving even more boldly. He marched into Austria and there repeated all the murderous and brutal methods which had given him power at home. Then he held a "free election" whereby the Austrians could say whether or not they wanted union with Germany. With German troops virtually occupying Austria, they naturally voted almost one hundred per cent for Hitler.

With the south secured—Mussolini stood just below Austria—Hitler looked to the southeast.

He saw Czechoslovakia.

This was the new state which the

The Growth of the Third Reich

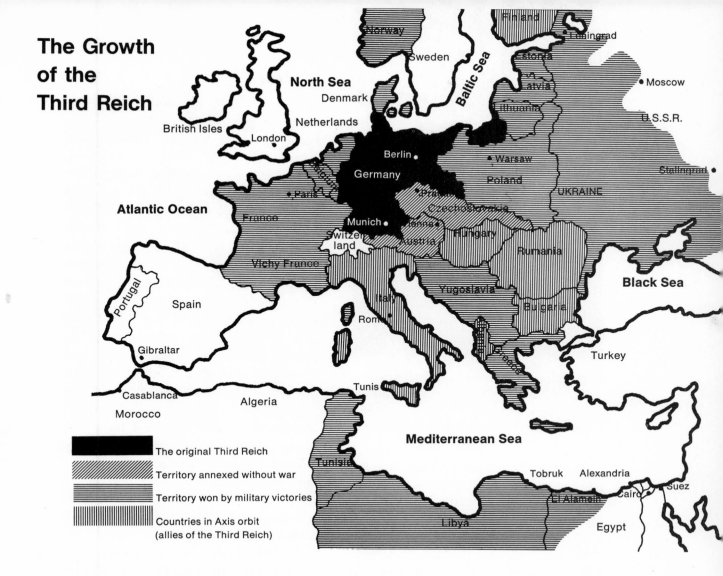

North Sea
Denmark
British Isles
London
Netherlands
Atlantic Ocean
France
Switzerland
Vichy France
Portugal
Spain
Gibraltar
Casablanca
Morocco
Algeria
Norway
Sweden
Baltic Sea
Finland
Leningrad
Estonia
Latvia
Lithuania
Moscow
U.S.S.R.
Berlin
Germany
Munich
Warsaw
Poland
UKRAINE
Stalingrad
Prague
Czechoslovakia
Vienna
Austria
Hungary
Rumania
Yugoslavia
Bulgaria
Black Sea
Rome
Italy
Greece
Turkey
Tunis
Mediterranean Sea
Tunisia
Tobruk
Alexandria
El Alamein
Cairo
Suez
Libya
Egypt

The original Third Reich

Territory annexed without war

Territory won by military victories

Countries in Axis orbit
(allies of the Third Reich)

Allies of World War I had set up and promised to protect. But they did not. Once again both England and France backed down before Hitler's demands. On September 29, 1938, at the famous Munich Conference, they agreed to allow Hitler to occupy the part of Czechoslovakia known as the Sudetenland. Hitler, a skillful liar, promised them that there would be no more land grabs in Europe. The next day Prime Minister Neville Chamberlain of Great Britain wrote out a pledge of friendship between Britain and Germany and asked Hitler to sign it. Hitler did.

Mr. Chamberlain waved this piece of paper when a cheering crowd greeted him on his return to London. He said it would bring "peace in our time." But Winston Churchill—one of the few Allied leaders who had warned the democracies of their peril—declared it would bring disaster. Churchill was right. Chamberlain had no sooner gone home than Hitler's agents were at work undermining the Czech government.

23

Sir Nevile Henderson, British ambassador to Berlin (left), Prime Minister Neville Chamberlain (center), and Hitler pose for photographers after the second of their historic conferences.

The Nazis manufactured a crisis, and the Czechoslovakian president, Emil Hacha, came to Berlin from the Czech capital in Prague to try to avert disaster. The Fuehrer shouted and yelled at him and made brutal threats. He told Hacha that German troops were on the march for Prague. He said the only thing Hacha could do to save his people was to order them not to fight. Hacha fainted. When he was revived, he telephoned Prague and said: "The fate of the Czech people . . . (is) trustingly in the hands of Der Führer."

On March 15, 1939, Hitler entered Prague in triumph. His southeastern frontier was now safe; a brave people and a mighty modern army were in his power, and with them the giant Skoda Works, one of the world's largest arsenals.

A shiver of dread ran through the democracies.

Before they had stopped shuddering, Hitler moved again, this time into Lithuania. He demanded the "return" of the Port of Memel on the Baltic Sea together with its surrounding area. He got it.

On April 7, the Allied nations received another blow. Mussolini invaded his little neighbor of Albania across the Adriatic Sea.

Now not only France and England were truly alarmed, but President Franklin Delano Roosevelt of the United States took a hand. He telegraphed Hitler and Mussolini asking them to promise no further aggression for ten "or even twenty-five years, if we are to look that far ahead."

Mussolini read the telegram and scornfully muttered, "Infantile paralysis!" This was a rude reference to the illness which had crippled President Roosevelt's legs. It had not, as Mussolini was to learn, affected the President's clear head and fighting heart.

In 1939, however, the Axis dictators were very sure of themselves. They had rightly guessed that the democracies' power to act was weakened by a spirit of appeasement. Appeasement—giving in to someone's demands in order to avoid trouble—was another of the seeds of World War I.

Why were the Allies so timid? Because they still had not forgotten the ordeal of World War I. They wanted peace, even "peace at any price." They shut their eyes while Hitler built the war machine which the Treaty of Versailles had forbidden him to have.

Meanwhile the smaller nations, seeing Germany strong and the Allies weak, became frightened. In 1936 little Belgium ended her alliance with France and declared herself neutral. In that way, Belgium hoped to avoid becoming the invasion route into France, as she had been in World War I. It was a foolish hope, but there was good reason for Belgium to attempt to secure her own safety.

The voices of such Allied leaders as Churchill, who warned the West of its peril, were mostly ignored. Instead, the voices that were heard were those of the appeasers and faint-hearted, who wanted "peace at any price," and of the misguided college students of the Oxford Union in England who passed the resolution, "That this House will in no circumstances fight for its King and Country."

Mussolini himself later said how much he was impressed by that shameful pledge. It convinced him that the English would not fight. Of the British nation of 1939, Mussolini said: "These men are not made of the same stuff as Francis Drake and the other magnificent English adventurers who created the Empire. They are, after all, the tired sons of a long line of rich men."

Hitler, too, was scornful. Nor did he believe that America would come to the aid of England and France again. "There's nobody more stupid than the Americans," he said. "I'll never believe the American soldier can fight like a hero."

Across the world in Tokyo similar talk about "the soft Americans" was coming from the Japanese generals and admirals. Their leader was General Hideki Tojo.

On the surface, there seemed to be much evidence to support this low estimate of the democracies' fighting spirit. Many Americans sincerely believed that their country should—and could— keep clear of Europe's troubles. They still regarded the two oceans as moats which kept the outer world at bay. They did not realize that the development of the airplane had ended this period of "isolation." Moreover, because the United States had not joined the

In celebration of one of Il Duce's visits to Germany, the Italian dictator and the Nazi Fuehrer inspect a guard of honor.

League of Nations, the League never had any real power to punish the Axis nations.

Early in 1939, however, the Allies became acutely aware of the danger. France prepared to mobilize her massive army, and both England and she let it be known that they would come to the aid of Poland if Hitler attacked.

Then on August 23, 1939, Hitler's Germany and Stalin's Russia signed a pact of friendship. The two great enemies—Nazism and Communism—had joined hands. The world could scarcely believe it. The significance of the pact was enormous. Hitler could now invade Poland without fear of opposition from Russia. And Hitler was determined to invade. He knew that he could bully the Allies no longer. The days of appeasement were over. He would have to fight for power, now, and the Allies were arming at such a rate that he had to strike before they became any stronger.

By August 22, Hitler had already made this decision known to his generals and admirals. Having gathered them together at the headquarters in Bavaria that he called his Eagle's Nest, he had told them:

"I shall give a propagandist reason for starting the war, no matter whether it is plausible or not. The victor will not be asked, later on, whether he told the truth or not. In . . . a war, it is not the Right that matters but Victory."

Hitler had ordered Himmler to fake an "incident" on the Polish border during the last night of August.

Next morning, the blitzkrieg was unleashed.

Fury in Finland | 5

After the fury of the blitzkrieg in Poland came the comedy of the "sitzkrieg" on the Western Front.

That was what soldiers jokingly called the six-month lull between the fall of Poland and the German attack on Norway and Denmark in April, 1940. It was "the sitdown war" or "the phony war." The British and French armies were entrenched behind the Maginot Line, while the Germans were gathered behind their Siegfried Line west of the Rhine. There was almost no combat.

On October 6 Hitler asked France and Britain to stop fighting. He said the Polish question had been "settled." But Chamberlain and Premier Edouard Daladier of France refused.

Meantime the soldiers of both sides faced each other and yawned. The British soldiers sang:

We're gonna hang out the washing
  on the Siegfried Line
If the Siegfried Line's still there.

All the military experts among the Allies began saying that a "war of attrition" had begun. Each side was trying to wear down the other side's ability to fight. It was believed that the Allies' superior industrial resources would carry the day. Between them, the British navy and the French army would be too much for Hitler.

This was foolish optimism which ignored the facts. First, Hitler had made massive preparations for war. The industrial machine he had built to supply his war machine was only then reaching its peak, and Hitler was using the lull to feed all of these hundreds of new tanks and airplanes into the mushrooming Wehrmacht. He was also moving his formations from east to west at this time.

Second, Hitler's Germany was not as isolated as the Kaiser's Germany had been. In World War I, Germany had fought a two-front war: against France, Britain, and the United States on the west, against Russia in the east. This time Russia was a friend and was sending supplies to Germany.

Russia herself was to cause most of the land action during the so-called phony war. Stalin's swoops began on the very day that the Nazis and Communists carved up Poland between them. On that day, the Russian Premier forced the tiny Baltic country of Estonia to grant Russia bases on Estonian soil. Within two weeks, the little Baltic states of Latvia and Lithuania were bullied into doing the same thing. Later on, Russia would take over these countries outright.

The greedy Russian bear was in for a surprise and a shock, however, when he tried the same bullying tactics on Finland. The brave Finns refused to sell or lease any of their land for a foreign

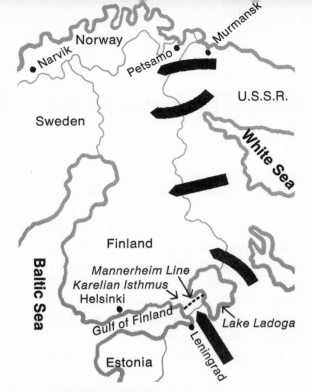

Russia Invades Finland

◀ Soviet Invasion Routes

military base. Russian newspapers began shouting that the ferocious Finns were preparing to attack peace-loving Russia. A nation of less than four million people proposing to invade one of more than a hundred and seventy million! It was, of course, mere propaganda—the pretext for the real Russian invasion of Finland that Stalin had scheduled.

On November 30, 1939, the Soviet army struck at Finland with 100,000 men moving along five invasion routes.

It was one of the most astonishing invasions in history. Many of the Russian soldiers were loaded down with propaganda leaflets and banners. Others marched gaily across the frontier behind brass bands. They expected to be welcomed as "liberators." They had believed their own propaganda. Worse, they were so certain of quick success that they wore only light clothing. They were not prepared for the bitter Finnish winter, nor were they equipped or trained for fighting in the Finnish forests or around the countless Finnish lakes. Far, far worse, they thought too little of their enemy.

Led by the famous Field Marshal Karl von Mannerheim, the Finns fought like tigers.

They fell back before the advancing Russian divisions, luring them deep into the forests and onto the frozen lakes. Then they struck. Cleverly shifting their attacks from column to column, the Finns would hit and hold the Russian front while other Finnish formations moved around to slash at the Russian flank. They cut off routes of retreat. They separated the Russian units from each other and chopped them up piecemeal. Finnish ski troops in white uniforms slipped over the snow like wraiths to pounce on the Russian rear. They ravaged supply columns, blew up roads, or set up ambushes in the murk of the forests. The Russians fell by the tens of thousands.

The world was amazed at the Finnish resistance. Britain and France began considering coming to Finland's rescue. In the United States there was wide admiration for Finland's stand.

Hitler was always aware that the Nazi-Communist alliance could not last and that he would one day have to fight Russia. Therefore he looked on his ally's disaster with interest and delight.

But Russia was appalled. By the end of the year not one of the five Soviet army columns had met any real success. Failure had overtaken the most important thrust, which had been made in the south against the Mannerheim Line. This was the defensive belt that the Finns had built on the Karelian Isthmus, which linked their country to Russia.

Stalin decided that the Mannerheim Line must be broken. It had to be done soon, for Stalin could understand the lesson that Hitler was drawing from the Russian debacle, and the West was getting ready to help the Finns. So Stalin called off the five-prong attack and massed all his forces opposite the Mannerheim Line. He was going to rely on Russia's fifty-to-one military superiority to crush Finnish resistance.

On February 1, blanket bombing of the Finnish rear by the Russian air force signaled the start of the second offensive. Then huge masses of artillery, lined up hub to hub, rained fire and steel on the Mannerheim Line. In a single twenty-four-hour period no less than three hundred thousand shells fell in this position. Then the Russian infantry attacked. In two weeks of fighting, the Mannerheim Line was breached. Forty-two days after the second offensive began, the gallant Finns capitulated.

Under the peace treaty, Russia acquired all that she had demanded, and more. She took Finland's second-biggest city, her biggest Arctic Ocean port, her biggest lake, and the whole Karelian Isthmus. This last grab proved to be important when the Germans later attacked Russia, for the Isthmus shielded the big Russian city of Leningrad.

Brave little Finland had fought until exhausted. She had lost 25,000 men killed, while inflicting more than 100,000 deaths on the invaders. Her defensive stand must rank among the most stirring in history.

A Russian soldier lying frozen beside captured Soviet tractor vehicles provides grim evidence of the bitter Finnish winter.

6 | Struggle at Sea

There never was a phony war at sea. From the very day that Britain declared war on Germany the navies of the Allies and the Axis became locked in a vast and vital sea duel.

It began on the night of September 3, 1939.

Standing about 250 miles off the coast of northwest Ireland, a German U-boat (*Unterseeboot*) began rising from the shadowy depths of the sea. Lieutenant Fritz-Julius Lemp raised his periscope above the surface. He stiffened. He had seen a British ship. It was to be his honor to strike the first blow in "The Battle of the Atlantic." (Actually the vessel was a British passenger liner, the *Athenia*.)

Lieutenant Lemp ordered the torpedo tubes loaded and fired. With a hissing of compressed air, four deadly "fish" flashed away toward the unsuspecting *Athenia*.

One of them struck. There was a rocking roar and the *Athenia* began to sink. Luckily she went down slowly, and quick rescue work saved all but 112 of the 1,417 persons aboard. Twenty-eight of these dead were Americans.

News of the sinking outraged the non-Axis world. The sinking of a civilian ship was in violation of international agreement. America was so angry that Germany tried to put the blame on Britain. The Nazis claimed that *Athenia* was sunk by a bomb secretly placed aboard her upon orders of Winston Churchill.

Churchill himself laughed at the lie, but he was still chilled by the news. He was now the First Lord of the Admiralty, in charge of the British Royal Navy and all British shipping. Since he had held the same post in World War I, no one was more aware than he of what a scourge the Nazi submarines could become.

In the First World War submarine warfare nearly brought Britain to her knees. Like sharks lurking in the depths, the deadly U-boats chewed Britain's life lines to bits. One of these life lines ran through the Mediterranean Sea and Suez Canal into the Indian and Pacific oceans. The other extended through the Atlantic to North and South America.

Allied ships along those life lines had been exposed to U-boat warfare during World War I, and they were just as naked now. Proof of this came in the next three days, during which the *Bosnia*, *Royal Sceptre*, and *Rio Claro*—all important ships—were torpedoed and sunk off the coast of Spain. In a week there were a dozen British ships on the bottom. Then the mighty aircraft carrier *Courageous* was sunk in the Bristol Channel.

By the end of the month losses were staggering. There was nothing for Churchill to do but to revive the scheme which had finally crushed the U-boat menace at the end of the First World War. This was the convoy system. Instead of sailing the seas singly as the submarines' helpless prey, the ships gathered in groups of from a half-dozen to dozens. They sailed at set speeds, escorted by destroyers. Much faster than the freighters and tankers or troop transports, the destroyers raced around and around the convoy, hunting for submarines. If they detected one submerged, the destroyers attacked by dropping depth charges—"ash cans," the sailors called them—off their stern. If they caught a U-boat on the surface, they tried to sink it with their deck guns.

Actually the convoy system was as much an offensive as a defensive weapon. It was the best way to get at the U-boats because the merchant ships acted as bait. Churchill revived this system, improving it by adding aircraft protection at either end of the voyage. It seemed successful. Although sixty-seven Allied merchantmen were lost in September-October, the Germans also lost twenty of their U-boats. Moreover they were hampered by a lack of bases. The French navy operating out of Dakar in Northwest Africa helped reduce the submarine threat. French warships also patrolled the Mediterranean and kept the Italian navy bottled up.

Then Allied sea fortunes sank again. On a dark October night a daring German submarine captain named Guenther Prien slipped into the great British naval base of Scapa Flow in the Orkney Islands off the north coast of Scotland. Captain Prien risked treacherous tides

With racks of depth charges fastened to its stern, a British destroyer keeps a lookout for enemy submarines and aircraft while patrolling a vast convoy in the Atlantic.

Oberleutnant Guenther Prien (left) salutes while a fellow officer congratulates every member of the submarine crew that sank the British battleship Royal Oak.

and currents and a narrow passage to penetrate British defenses and torpedo the battleship *Royal Oak*. The great ship capsized immediately and more than two-thirds of those aboard perished.

There was worse to come.

British ships began to blow up and sink as they entered or left port. The Germans were dropping a new type of mine at the harbor mouths. It was a magnetic mine, drawn to a ship's steel hull as the vessel passed over it. This was a dreadful weapon. While incoming and outgoing ships began to blow up and sink in staggering numbers, the British Admiralty frantically tried to locate a magnetic mine for study.

Late in November, 1939, came the breathless news that a low-flying German airplane had been seen dropping a mine off the British coast. The mine had fallen in mud flats which would be exposed when the tide receded.

Two skilled and courageous naval officers were rushed to the area. In darkness, armed only with a signal lamp, they ventured out on the mud. They found the mine imbedded there. But the tide was rising, and they had to return to land. Next day they made a second trip to the mine. Working carefully—the slightest slip would mean not only their own end but the end of their golden opportunity—they disarmed the mine.

It was brought back to Portsmouth Naval Base in triumph. And the Royal Navy put its cleverest scientists to work piercing the mysteries of Hitler's secret weapon. As soon as they had analyzed its characteristics, they were able to work out methods of combating it. All types of British ships were demagnetized by encircling them with an electric cable. This technique was called "degaussing." Shipping losses declined, and fear of the magnetic mine faded.

But a new threat appeared in the presence of German surface warships. Chief among them were the pocket battleships *Deutschland, Admiral Scheer,* and *Admiral Graf Spee,* and the battle cruisers *Scharnhorst* and *Gneisenau.* The three pocket battleships were the most formidable. German naval engineers had been amazingly successful in putting a battleship's punch aboard a cruiser's frame.

It was not that Hitler's navy could challenge the Royal Navy. In tonnage alone the British outweighed the Germans 2,000,000 tons to 235,000 tons. But Hitler hoped to turn his pocket battleships loose on the British shipping lanes as raiders. And he intended to use the battle cruisers for sudden swoops on the British blockade line of armed merchant cruisers.

As such, Hitler's ships were always a threat to the Royal Navy. The British Admiralty's fondest hope was to bring the German warships to battle and sink them.

In late November, a British merchant cruiser on patrol south of Iceland sighted a big warship bearing down on her rapidly. Although she thought it was the powerful *Deutschland,* she opened fire anyhow, hoping to draw bigger British ships than herself to the scene. The German ship was not *Deutschland.* Instead, it turned out to be the battle cruisers *Scharnhorst* and *Gneisenau,* only one of which was visible. Between them they battered the gallant British ship into a blazing wreck.

But a British cruiser had seen the gun flashes and was rushing to the battle, followed by another. They pursued the German battle twins, losing sight of them in darkness and a heavy rain. In its eagerness the Royal Navy fed more and more ships into the pursuit until fourteen cruisers were engaged. But their prey eluded them, slipping through the British blockade line off Norway during thick weather. The German warships reëntered the Baltic Sea.

The Royal Navy was embarrassed. There was even criticism of Churchill.

Worse than this failure to avenge the loss of the merchant cruiser and to remove a threat to the blockade line was the disturbing news from the South Atlantic. The pocket battleship *Graf Spee* was ravaging British shipping like a wolf among sheep. *Graf Spee* was an 11-inch warship; that is, her biggest guns measured eleven inches in diameter and could fire shells weighing more than a thousand pounds. She had left Germany

before the war, thereby eluding the British blockade, and had sailed to the Atlantic coast of South America. In two months she sank nine vessels.

Considered one of the most beautiful fighting ships afloat—with her strong lean lines and the clean unbroken sweep of her main deck—she was an awesome sight to enemy ships the moment she closed upon them with her 11-inch guns spouting orange flame and shrieking steel. As soon as she had disposed of her prey, *Graf Spee* would vanish into those trackless ocean wastes from which she had burst. Only the convulsed water above her victim's watery grave testified to her terrible presence.

The British Admiralty tried to bring *Graf Spee* to battle. But her skillful commander, Captain Hans Langsdorff, eluded all the Royal Navy's teams of hunters. His mission was to prey on weaker vessels—unarmed tankers and cargo ships. To accept battle with British fighting ships would jeopardize this mission. Nevertheless, Langsdorff had an able opponent in Commodore Henry Harwood of the Royal Navy.

Harwood decided that *Graf Spee*

(Left) Captain Hans Langsdorff of the Graf Spee. *(Right) Admiral Sir Henry Harwood, who led the chase after the German warship.*

would one day come to the area off Rio de Janeiro in Brazil because shipping was so heavy there. He put his force of four cruisers in that vicinity. On December 2 he heard that *Graf Spee* had claimed another victim, the *Doric Star*, at a point 3,000 miles away. Commodore Harwood made the shrewd guess that the German raider would now head for waters off Rio de Janeiro. Calculating that she would arrive near the River Plate by December 13, he ordered his four cruisers to steam there. Unluckily his 8-inch cruiser *Cumberland* was refitting in port. But he still had the 8-inch *Exeter* and the 6-inch *Ajax* and *Achilles*.

By the twelfth this plucky trio stood outside the mouth of the River Plate, which separates Argentina from Uruguay. They were ready to intercept the mighty *Graf Spee*.

Shortly after six o'clock on the morning of December 13, smoke was sighted to the east.

It was *Graf Spee*. She was approaching at full speed.

Captain Langsdorff's lookouts quickly sighted the British cruisers. But Langsdorff thought he had to deal with only a light cruiser and two destroyers. He came on. Then he realized his mistake. Even so, he did not hold off in order to give himself a chance to batter the Britishers with his 11-inchers before they could get him in range. He came charging on, the sharp prow of the *Graf Spee* knifing the water and a great bow wave spreading away from her.

Almost simultaneously, the British and German gunners opened fire. The *Exeter's* 8-inch shells struck the German

raider. And *Graf Spee* scored a hit with her heavier 11-inchers *Exeter* was badly out of control for a time. But *Ajax* and *Achilles*, with their 6-inch guns, had *Graf Spee* in range. They raked the big German. *Graf Spee* swung its biggest gun turrets on the smaller Britishers, thus allowing *Exeter* to repair some of the damage done to her. Now all three of Commodore Harwood's cruisers were battering *Graf Spee*. Wounded, the great ship let off smoke and turned away under this screen. Langsdorff was making for the mouth of the Plate.

But the British cruisers prevented his escape. Infuriated, Langsdorff let all of *Graf Spee's* big guns come to bear on the limping *Exeter*. They battered her unmercifully. But the gallant Captain Bell refused to pull out of the battle. Not until his last gun turret was put out of action did Bell finally turn away. This withdrawal came only after one hour and twenty-five minutes of steady battle.

Graf Spee was far from free, though. Harwood in *Ajax* led his flagship and her sister ship, *Achilles*, in dogged pursuit of the big German, now steaming hard south for Montevideo. The *Graf Spee* battered them both. Under cover of smoke, the British cruisers turned away. The *Graf Spee* did not pursue. She continued south, and the Britishers turned about and hung grimly on her stern. Shortly after midnight, *Graf Spee* entered the neutral harbor of Montevideo, Uruguay. She lay there repairing her damage and taking off wounded. The next night the *Cumberland* joined *Ajax* and *Achilles* on patrol off the harbor mouth.

The Graf Spee *in flames off Montevideo.*

Langsdorff became alarmed. The neutral government of Uruguay was already indicating that if he did not leave port soon it would intern his ship and his crew. Langsdorff telegraphed the German admiralty for advice. A conference presided over by Hitler was held, after which Langsdorff was sent this message:

"Attempt by all means to extend the time in neutral waters. . . . Fight your way through to Buenos Aires if possible. No internment in Uruguay. Attempt effective destruction if ship is scuttled."

But Uruguay would not permit Langsdorff to stall for time. Sorrowfully, the German captain decided he must scuttle his ship; that is, sink it himself. He had overestimated the power of the British force outside the port and thought that if he tried to break through he would surely lose. If so his ship might be captured. Fearing to have some of *Graf Spee's* secret equipment fall into enemy hands, Langsdorff took the great ship out into the port's deep water and blew her up.

Two days later he wrapped himself in the old Imperial German flag—an insult to Hitler and his swastika—and shot himself.

So ended the first phase of The Battle of the Atlantic. By the end of 1939 the Allies appeared to have the sea situation well in hand. Yet by the summer of 1940 it would be woefully out of hand again, for in the spring of that year the phony war ended for good.

7 | Swastika over Norway

In war the objective is to destroy the enemy's power to fight or his will to fight. But to destroy the enemy's power it is vitally necessary to have bases— bases from which armies form and march, ships load and sail, and airplanes fly.

During the opening blows of the sea struggle, the British and French possessed most of the naval bases. These enabled the Allies to control the seas and bottle up the German and Italian fleets.

To counteract this superiority of the Allies, Hitler hurled his second lightning bolt of World War II against neutral Norway and Denmark. He wanted Norway's coast for submarine bases, and he wanted to control the Skaggerak passage from the Baltic into the open North Atlantic. More, he wanted these before Britain got them.

Britain, of course, had no intention of violating Norway's neutrality. She had not done so even when it meant she could not come to Finland's rescue through Norway. And she had continued to respect Norwegian neutrality even when she saw Swedish iron ore—vital to Germany—come down through Norwegian territorial waters guarded by Norwegian coastal craft.

Hitler, however, was no respecter of any nation's neutrality. He had already said openly that might makes right. And in February of 1940 he determined to seize Norway and Denmark for himself. He had become alarmed over the affair of the *Altmark*.

The *Altmark* was the auxiliary supply ship of the sunken *Graf Spee*. And she had taken aboard prisoners from Allied ships which the *Graf Spee* had destroyed. In February, 1940, *Altmark* was sighted by the British in Norwegian waters. A flotilla of British vessels pursued her and cornered her in a sea inlet. Norwegian authorities said she had been inspected twice and had no prisoners. The British doubted this. After the *Altmark* tried to escape by ramming the British destroyer *Cossack*, the *Cossack* came alongside her. A British boarding party leaped onto the *Altmark's* decks and conquered the ship in a sharp hand-to-hand fight. Below, battened down in storerooms, about three hundred British prisoners were found by the rescuers.

Hitler considered this "violation" of Norwegian neutrality sufficient proof that Britain intended to invade Norway. He promptly gathered forces to carry out his own invasion plans, which he had begun to draw up as far back as December. On April 8, 1940, after Britain informed Norway that she was going to mine her coastal waters, Hitler issued this statement:

"Icily cold, Germany watches these developments. Icily cold, Germany watches the unfolding of the drama. Icily cold, Germany reserves her own

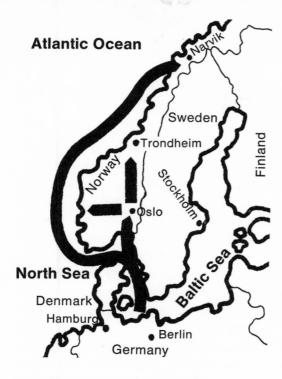

Atlantic Ocean

Narvik

Sweden

●Trondheim

Norway

Finland

Stockholm

●Oslo

Baltic Sea

North Sea

Denmark

Hamburg

●Berlin
Germany

Germany Invades Scandinavia

◄ German Invasion Points

decisions to meet the situation."

Next day the invasion began.

It came without warning, as usual. Nazi armor rolled over the Danish frontier, and Nazi agents cut off Denmark from the world. Within a few hours the German spearheads were in the capital city of Copenhagen. In twenty-four hours Denmark had been conquered.

But Norway offered resistance. Here the Germans had again stunned the world with the power, precision, and speed of their attack. Once more the Luftwaffe cleared the way. Then came paratroopers dropped at five important port cities. Next, warships led troop transports into all the important ports along the entire coast, and the helmeted Nazi assault troops began battling inland.

Though the German land fighting was to prove victorious, the German navy got a bloody nose at Oslo. Grand Admiral Erich Raeder had sent the pocket battleship *Deutschland* and cruisers *Emden* and *Bluecher*, together with training ship *Brummer*, to Oslo. A fleet of smaller craft accompanied them.

Against the German vessels was only a little mine layer named after the medieval Norwegian warrior, Olav Tryggvason, along with two minesweepers. These were backed up by Oslo's coastal batteries.

Bold little *Olav Tryggvason* sank a German minesweeper and held off two destroyers and damaged cruiser *Emden*. Then the shore batteries opened up and sank *Bluecher* and *Brummer* outright, damaging *Emden* still further and wounding big *Deutschland*. It was a gallant defensive, and Oslo was taken only by parachute landings and flanking seaborne attacks in the inlets.

Up at the important northern port of Narvik, the Germans attacked with guile and power. For a week supposedly empty German ore boats had been moving up to Narvik. Secretly loaded with ammunition and supplies, they anchored to await the German troops. These swept into the bay aboard ten destroyers led by *Scharnhorst* and *Gneisenau*. The German ships fell on the two small Norwegian warships in the bay and sank them in a brief battle.

After this Narvik was overwhelmed.

To the south, Norway's other major ports were also falling.

Hitler's second invasion was becoming a striking success. It had been launched

In a Norwegian harbor Nazi soldiers disembark from a German warship.

from sea and sky, always more difficult than over land, as in Poland. But the victory was not due to military prowess alone. Two enemies from without—German propaganda and German sabotage—had confused and paralyzed Norway. And the enemy within—traitors—had betrayed her.

Vidkun Quisling was the chief traitor. Once the port cities fell, he seized the radio and presented himself as the pro-German ruler of Norway. His name has since gone into many languages as the synonym for traitor, and he was executed by his countrymen after the fall of Hitler.

Loyal Norwegians treated Quisling's broadcast with anger and disdain. The King and government fled from Oslo and took to the hills. Patriots seized arms and joined them. Pursued by German armored cars and airplanes, they were machine-gunned and bombed, while the rest of the country was cowed into submission by calculated brutality.

King Haakon appealed to Britain for help.

A rescue force was hastily scraped together and sent to the vicinity of Trondheim in central Norway and Narvik in the north.

At Trondheim the British force was cut to pieces by the Nazis. The would-be rescuers had been dumped into snow and deep mud without adequate clothing, without artillery, without airplanes or antiaircraft guns to protect them. In four days, half of them were dead. Six days later the rest were withdrawn.

At Narvik, the British took the port. But then they had to give it up. Once again the power of the Luftwaffe made it clear that men on foot—even ships at sea—cannot fight without friendly control of the air. The only British success in the entire operation came after the British battleship *Warspite* broke into the harbor at Narvik and pounded seven enemy destroyers beneath the waves.

Even so, the British lost the aircraft carrier *Glorious* and two destroyers to the guns of *Scharnhorst* and *Gneisenau* on June 8—the last day of action since the British forces were withdrawn.

Hitler had won again. In fact, he had been so confident of victory that he had hurled his third lightning bolt while the Battle of Norway was still raging. A month earlier he had invaded neutral Belgium, Holland, and Luxembourg.

And with this third stroke, Adolf Hitler had brought into the field against him the man he hated most in the world —Winston Churchill. The German invasion of the Low Countries, Belgium and Holland, had caused Prime Minister Chamberlain to resign. Churchill took his place. On May 13, 1940, he spoke to Parliament, saying: "I have nothing to offer but blood, toil, tears, and sweat.

. . . Come, then, let us go forward together with our united strength."

A thrill of hope ran through the British people. It was typical of them to feel the joy of battle when all seemed lost. Churchill knew this. This is why he had the great courage and the audacity to talk of "victory," when across the Channel the heaviest blows of all were beginning to fall.

Hitler's troops advance through a flaming Norwegian village.

8 | France Falls

The night of May 9, 1940, Dutch Intelligence received a secret message from agents inside Germany.

"Tomorrow at dawn," the agents warned. "Hold tight!"

The Dutch thought they were prepared for the surprise attack the next morning. They planned to slow down the enemy until help could come from the massive army assembled in the south by France and England. To do this they were going to open the dikes and let the sea flow in to engulf the invader. Canal sluices would be opened, too. It was believed that by pressing a few buttons the long frontier of Holland could be turned into impassable watery wastes. Then the mined bridges would be blown up. The Dutch soldiery, meanwhile, would wait behind roadblocks and inside pillboxes covering the vital road nets.

It was false confidence. In a single day, the onrushing Germans pierced the Dutch defenses and seized the entire frontier.

They came before the dawn, out of the dark with a sudden rush. Parachutists were dropped in large numbers near the dikes and canals. Some of them wore Allied uniforms, or the uniforms of Dutch policemen, postmen, or railway conductors. They were equipped with machine guns and radios, and carried rubber boats for crossing canals and flooded areas. The paratroopers jumped from very low levels and many of them were drowned or hit the ground with killing impact. But there were many more, enough to seize the canal locks and water controls, or to capture footholds for later bridging operations.

On the unflooded lowlands the tank columns slashed through Dutch resistance, swarming over the countryside like mechanical vermin.

Once again the Luftwaffe knocked out the enemy air force. Screaming Stukas made their devilish dives on Dutch nerve centers. Defenseless Rotterdam—declared an "open city" by the Dutch—was deliberately bombed into ruins to terrify the Dutch people.

And then the German infantry began battling forward to link up with the faster-moving mechanized forces and parachutists who had carved out friendly islands in the demoralized Dutch rear.

Holland fell in five days.

This was five times better than tiny Luxembourg, which had scarcely a squad of men to defend it. Luxembourg, attacked on the same morning as Holland, went down in a day.

Belgium held out longest.

For a few days, the world thrilled to the Belgian defense, believing that these doughty people were to repeat their valiant stand of World War I.

This was not to be. The "invincible" Belgian fort of Eben Emael was taken with surprising ease. The German

One of the many German paratroopers dropped into the Netherlands.

soldiers who conquered it had trained for months on just this one mission. There were only 150 of them. They emerged out of the darkness above the fort in Luftwaffe gliders. Landing silently on Eben Emael's flat roof, they made smokescreens and raced to work.

Moving like robots, they rushed from big gun to big gun—dropping explosives down their muzzles. They blew up exits and observation posts. They tossed grenades into the ammunition elevators and ruined these, too. Then they began dropping explosives down ventilation shafts and gun slits.

They sat on top of the world's strongest fort and calmly awaited its surrender.

No one could get to them for the

Luftwaffe controlled the skies. After Eben Emael's commander appealed to neighboring forts for help, his codefenders responded by opening fire on Eben Emael. The idea was to blast the Nazis off the roof. But the Germans took cover, stepping up their grenade-dropping during the lulls. Eben Emael surrendered less than a day after it was assaulted.

Meanwhile, French and British forces—supported by Polish formations who had escaped to fight again—began to move north toward Belgium. They hoped to stem the German tide and establish a fixed position from which they might launch their counteroffensive.

But on May 13—only three days after

The Blitzkrieg Strikes the Low Countries

◀ German Invasion Points

the invasion began—a German general named Ewald von Kleist achieved the "impossible." His tanks came through the rugged Ardennes forests of Belgium. The Allied generals had thought that no large bodies of tanks could get through these hilly woods. They had been confident that their right flank was safe. But von Kleist's Panzers or armored units tore a hole fifty miles wide in the Allied right flank. Tanks and armored cars poured through. They took off in a wild, clanking, fighting dash for the Channel coast, reaching it in just seven days.

The French and British forces were cut in two!

Back in Germany Adolf Hitler exulted at the news. "The Fuehrer is beside himself with joy," one of his generals wrote in his diary.

And no wonder. The British Expeditionary Force, including some French troops and the Poles, was being driven back toward the Channel. They had their backs to the water. Under the steady blows of the Germans, the British were being herded into a pocket that might at any moment be turned into a slaughter pen.

A momentous and agonizing decision was being forced upon Prime Minister Churchill not two weeks after he had taken up the reins of leadership. Should he order his men to fight on, or try to get them out?

Belgium made up his mind for him. On May 28, King Leopold — a leader without the fighting qualities his father had displayed in the First World War— gave up despite the pleas of his Allies.

The Belgian Army surrendered.

As a result, the British situation had become impossible. German spearheads were already lunging at their pocket from the south and from the west. Now the entire weight of German might in Belgium might fall upon them from the north.

Winston Churchill did not delay. He ordered the evacuation he had already prepared. The Allied forces were to be drawn out of the trap. They were to be rescued by water in that glorious operation known as the miracle of Dunkirk.

The British Expeditionary Force was retreating into the little French city of Dunkirk on the Channel coast in an orderly pullback. First, the British "Tommies" destroyed what equipment they could to keep it out of German hands, although they had to leave an enormous amount intact. Then the units fought and fell back, fought and fell back, like backward leapfrogging. The French fought two fierce delaying actions at Lille and Cassel to help.

Nevertheless, the Germans closed in— exultant and lusting for the kill.

Overhead were the buzzing, growling Stukas and Messerschmitts of the Luftwaffe. They strafed the troops and unloaded their deadly eggs. The soft Dunkirk sand smothered the German bombs, but even so, the Tommies kept asking each other: "Where is the R.A.F.?" They didn't know that the fighter pilots of the Royal Air Force—though high above and out of sight—were locked in deadly duels with the enemy fliers. Fighting for days without relief, they kept the Luftwaffe from turning Dunkirk into a

British troops move through a Dunkirk street, heading for the ships that will take them back to England. Victims of the bombardment lie in the street.

bloody turkey shoot.

And across the English Channel streamed the strangest armada in history. It was almost a civilian fleet coming to rescue the military from disaster. Of the 887 vessels used in the evacuation of Dunkirk, 665 of them were civilian. It was a scarecrow of a fleet, too, a ragtail bobtail fleet: large boats and small; slender or squat; motor-driven, sail-driven, oar-driven. There were motorboats and lifeboats, fishing boats and pleasure boats, yachts and yawls and Channel ferries. There were lifeboats, destroyers and drifters; excursion boats and little passenger liners and tugs towing barges; paddle wheelers, fireboats, tramp steamers, French ketches, and Dutch *schuits* and one car ferry making its first voyage on the open sea.

They sailed toward the enormous pall of smoke hanging like an umbrella over Dunkirk, while around them warships formed a defensive ring to fill the air with ack-ack and enlarge the pall.

It was a kind of chaos on the Channel. Destroyers dashing in and out of this motley fleet to keep order sometimes created waves that nearly capsized smaller boats. Ships were constantly colliding, for there was very little room to maneuver. Yet out of this chaos came order.

Small boats put into beaches black with troops. Men standing shoulder high in water clambered aboard or were hauled aboard. The boats carried the men out to the ships, while other boats took their place. The men in waist-deep water had already moved to shoulder depth. Their places were taken by men standing knee deep. And so it went for a solid week. Scorning the bombs and bullets of the enemy, unhurried by the approaching sound of German artillery,

43

Along the beach at Dunkirk, men wade out to small rescue craft.

the sailors and civilians of this scare-crow fleet saved the British Expedition-ary Force. They brought 338,226 men from France to England. Of these, 198,-315 were British and 139,911 were French, Polish and Belgian.

Hitler heard the news and raged in frustration. He had hoped for annihila-tion or complete surrender. Britain could not very easily have survived the loss of all her veteran troops and commanders. She would have been powerless against the cross-Channel invasion which Hitler hoped to launch immediately after the fall of France.

And France was falling.

Fast motorized German columns had wheeled south from the vicinity of the Ardennes breakthrough and were sweep-ing down toward Paris. It was only a matter of time. All over stunned and sorrowing France long, ragged columns of French soldiers were being led away

to prison cages. Their rifles were stacked on the roads and ground to pieces by tanks.

Mechanized spearheads clattered into silent and hostile French villages. Their officers stood in open turrets shouting, "Heil Hitler!" and taunting the villagers with the stiff-armed Nazi salute.

It was as though France had lost the power to resist. Once again the world was shown the truth of the saying that generals are always trying to fight the new war with the tactics of the old. The French army had prepared itself for the old-fashioned position warfare fought out by huge entrenched armies in the First World War. They were not ready for Hitler's lightning war. French gen-erals had become defense-minded. They relied too heavily on their Maginot Line. They forgot that the Maginot Line was just one part of the overall defense plan. Its purpose was to block the enemy in the east and force him to attack in the open north. Then in the north the French generals would fight the enemy with one part of their troops and keep another part "in reserve." The reserve troops would be rushed from place to place, wherever the danger was greatest.

But when the blitzkrieg began smashing south, the French army had no reserve. All the troops were on the battle line. When the German breakthrough came, there were no spare soldiers to rush into the breach.

Nor did the French make good use of their tanks. They scattered their armored divisions instead of massing them to meet the German assault. The light French tanks which went up against the heavy Panzer units were quickly knocked out. One of the most heartbreaking messages of the war was the postcard received by the new French premier, Paul Reynaud, from a French officer who had committed suicide. It said:

"I am killing myself, M. Premier, to let you know that all my men were brave, but one cannot send men to fight tanks with rifles."

This was what was happening, and after the Luftwaffe beat down Anglo-French resistance in the skies, the collapse became complete.

Then came panic.

The great and valorous French nation suddenly seemed to go flabby with fear. Hundreds of thousands of French civilians had already been clogging the roads in a mass flight from the northern battlefront. They had been deliberately driven south by the Luftwaffe's terrify-ing attacks. They had flowed through Paris, and had infected that great city with their fear. Now, out of beautiful Paris, under the hot June sun, came an outpouring of frightened humanity upon whom the Luftwaffe fell like fiendish vultures.

Everyone and everything was put to the bullet or the bomb: human beings young or old, horses, automobiles, farm wagons, and carts. The roads south of Paris became the corridors of the damned. All along them there echoed the wailing of women and children, the cursing of men, the whine of changing gears, or the sudden squeal of braked tires and the thud of colliding vehicles. And all of this racket was punctuated by the roar of German bombers flashing by at treetop level to add the crash of bombs and the screams of the stricken to the symphony of suffering.

At this point Mussolini rushed to join the kill. On June 10 Italy declared war on France, and the Italian army began invading southern France.

From across the sea came the scornful voice of President Roosevelt, saying: "The hand that held the dagger has struck it into the back of its neighbor."

Two days later, Winston Churchill flew to the city of Tours—to which the French government had fled. He pleaded with the French to continue the fight. But a stunned spirit of defeat had gripped France's leaders. Only a colonel named Charles de Gaulle seemed still unbowed. But this tall, proud man of destiny had no power or influence at that time. After Churchill promised that England would continue to fight, no

German occupation troops in Paris pass beneath the Arc de Triomphe.

matter what, General Maxime Weygand looked at him with a sad smile and said: "You have a very good antitank obstacle." He meant the English Channel, and by this remark he indicated that France thought there was no hope of halting the rampaging German tanks.

On June 14 the Germans entered Paris. They found a deserted city. The next day they paraded in triumph on the Place de la Concorde.

"All is lost!" Premier Reynaud cried. He appealed to President Roosevelt for "clouds of airplanes." But this was not possible.

On June 16, with the French front cracking everywhere, Churchill proposed a union of France and England as a single country. By this he hoped to encourage his ally to fight on. The offer was refused. Marshal Pétain, the aged hero of Verdun in World War I, was now in power. He was a defeatist. On June 17 Marshal Pétain announced to a stunned France: "It is futile to continue the struggle against an enemy

Hitler dances a little jig of victory at Compiègne.

superior in numbers and in arms. It is with a heavy heart that I say we must cease the fight."

Pétain had surrendered without asking for terms!

Many Frenchmen found such disgrace unbearable. They began to go into hiding, organizing the famous French Underground which fought the Nazis throughout the war. Colonel Charles de Gaulle decided to preserve French honor by escaping to England to rally the Free French from there.

On June 21 Adolf Hitler arrived in Compiègne. There he danced a little jig of victory. Compiègne was the very place at which Kaiser Wilhelm's Ger-

many had accepted the terms of the World War I Armistice. Hitler intended to avenge this humiliation by making the French surrender at the same place and inside the same railway car where French Marshal Foch had dictated the Armistice. This was done the next day.

France was cut in two, with the north part occupied by Germany and the south run by Marshal Pétain with a capital at Vichy. This became known as the "Vichy Government" and was hated by most loyal Frenchmen for its policy of assisting the Germans.

In Berlin huge crowds of exultant Germans heard the news and began singing, "We Sail against England."

9 | The Battle of Britain

Adolf Hitler hoped that he would not have to invade England.

The Fuehrer knew that a war with the British would be hard and bloody. Moreover, he wanted to enjoy the triumph of his victories on the Continent. He made a speech suggesting that Britain quit the war and leave western Europe in Nazi hands.

The British coldly brushed aside Hitler's "peace offer." The Fuehrer should have known better.

The very day that the Dunkirk armada completed its dramatic rescue, Winston Churchill had delivered his historic fighting speech. He said:

"We shall fight on the seas and oceans, we shall fight with growing confidence and growing strength in the air, we shall defend our island, whatever the cost may be, we shall fight on the beaches, we shall fight on the landing-grounds, we shall fight in the fields and in the streets, we shall fight in the hills; we shall never surrender."

Right after this, in another irony of the war, the British attacked the fleet of their fallen ally, France. Fearing that this splendid instrument of war might fall into Nazi hands, a British fleet sailed to Oran in Algeria and destroyed three big battleships and damaged another in a brief, fierce gun battle. Other ships were disarmed in Egypt and the French West Indies, and a battleship was damaged at Dakar in French Northwest Africa.

The Fuehrer now decided he would have to invade England. He had to do it before winter—not only because of the weather, but because Hitler believed he had to conquer England before the United States entered the war against him.

Storm signals were already flying in America. Even before France fell, the United States Congress had voted a huge sum of money to build a "two-ocean navy." All the American armed forces were growing. The first peacetime draft of servicemen in the history of the

Prime Minister Winston Churchill who, with his cigar and his "V for Victory" sign, came to symbolize the British "bulldog breed."

United States was being prepared, and the fires of energy had been lighted beneath the giant industrial generator which is America. Supplies were already pouring into England.

But if Hitler could conquer Britain in time, he would make Germany so powerful that America would not dare move against him.

In late July, Hitler ordered the invasion of England. Grand Admiral Erich Raeder said right away that the German navy wasn't strong enough to conduct a channel crossing under the guns of the British navy. He also reminded Hitler that the losses of warships in Norway had crippled his fleet. But the Fuehrer insisted that the invasion plan—Operation Sea Lion—be put in action. The Germans planned to cross the Channel at its narrowest point. Troops would sail across a corridor between two thick fields of mines. Submarines would patrol on either side of this lane.

Sea Lion, of course, depended on the Luftwaffe's wresting control of the British skies from the Royal Air Force. Marshal Goering promised that his pilots would destroy the R.A.F. Boastful and overconfident as always, Goering also assured Hitler that his Luftwaffe alone could beat the British. He would rain death and destruction on the English cities and bomb the British to their knees. Hitler told him to go ahead, and the great aerial conflict known as the Battle of Britain began.

In the five weeks between Dunkirk and the opening of the Battle of Britain, the British turned their island into a bristling hedgehog of defense.

Antiaircraft guns were put in position. Huge barrage balloons were floated overhead. Beaches were barricaded and fortified. Buildings were sandbagged. Trenches were dug right across golf courses or back yards if it was decided that this was necessary to defend a certain road junction or power plant. Troops who had escaped at Dunkirk were rearmed, many with World War I weapons sent from America. A Civil Defense Service was organized. This included fire-fighting units, repair groups, and demolition squads. Everyone did duty as a fire-watcher, for every person and penny in the island was now at the government's disposal. Then a Home Guard of about a million older men was organized, and factories went on round-the-clock schedules to turn out guns and airplanes.

By July 10, 1940—the day the Battle of Britain began—the Royal Air Force had climbed to a strength of 1,475 front-line planes for home defense. Against this, Goering had 2,670 front-line aircraft. In quality, the British and German planes were about even. The Luftwaffe's were faster with a better rate of climb; the British craft were better armed and more maneuverable. Since control of the skies is generally determined, in the end, by fighter planes, the Battle of Britain was to be fought by German Messerschmitts against British Spitfires and Hurricanes.

Goering had one big advantage: The German conquests gave the Luftwaffe many forward bases in the west of Europe. These bases were widely scattered,

An umbrella of barrage balloons, similar to the one above, protected British cities from dive-bombing attacks by the Luftwaffe. Here, members of the Women's Auxiliary Air Force (WAAFs) are manipulating the guy ropes, as they raise the balloon aloft.

and thus hard for Britain's Bomber Command to attack. Also, the Germans could mass great numbers against the bunched-up British bases, and make feints to deceive their enemy. British scientists, however, had developed ra-

R.A.F. pilots relax between alerts, ready to dash to their planes at a moment's notice.

dar. This was an electronic device which could "see" vast distances. Radar equipment could detect objects such as airplanes while they were very far away; it could actually measure how far away they were. Thus, before the German planes reached their target, British airplanes could be sent into the air to intercept them. And ground troops could man their antiaircraft guns.

England's greatest single asset was the tenacity of her people. They were truly "the bulldog breed." From the man who looked like John Bull himself —Prime Minister Churchill—came the great rallying cry:

"Upon this battle depends the survival of Christian civilization. Upon it depends our British life, and the long continuity of our institutions and our Empire. The whole fury and might of the enemy must very soon be turned on us. Hitler knows that he will have to break us in this island or lose the war. If we can stand up to him, all Europe may be free and the life of the world may move forward into broad, sunlit uplands. But if we fail, then the whole world, including the United States, including all that we have known and cared for, will sink into the abyss of a new Dark Age, made more sinister, and perhaps more protracted, by the lights of perverted science.

"Let us therefore brace ourselves to our duties and so bear ourselves that, if the British Empire and its Commonwealth last for a thousand years, men will still say, 'This was their finest hour.' "

The Battle of Britain began over the

A Hurricane squadron, followed by Spitfires, climbs through the clouds to intercept an enemy formation reported heading for London.

Channel and the south of England. The German pilots attacked Channel shipping and ports in an effort to draw the R.A.F. fighters into the battles that would sweep them from the skies. The young British fliers took up the challenge with a skill and light-hearted daring that commanded the world's admiration. These were the youths of the very generation which had produced the Oxford Pledge not to fight for King or Country. They had been taunted as "softies." Now, rising in their Spitfires and Hurricanes—aided by Polish, French, Czech, Belgian, and Canadian fliers and American volunteers—they redeemed their honor.

For weeks on end dogfights raged above the clouds. People stood on rooftops anxiously seeking a glimpse of the combat. But they rarely saw it. They could only hear the growling of the motors, the screeching of protesting wings in steep dives, the stuttering of machine guns or the booming of wing cannon, and sometimes the tinkling sound of empty cartridges striking the streets and buildings below. But then, suddenly, out of the unseen melee a stricken plane would come plummeting. Its fall would be straight and swift, its passage marked by smoke trails drawing a smudge across the sky. And then it would crash in plumes of fire. If it fell into the Channel, it sent geysers of white water leaping skyward.

From his stand in the street a newspaper vendor watches a dogfight raging overhead.

The British cheered to see how often the planes with black German crosses were falling. They bowed their heads in silent prayer or looked away in anguish if the falling plane had the British bull's-eye on its fuselage.

Thus the Battle of Britain seesawed back and forth into mid-August. Steadily, their own sense of victory rising, the R.A.F. fliers whittled down the numerically superior enemy. But Goering did not realize that this was happening. His

51

war birds exaggerated their success, and he believed them. The Marshal decided that he had drawn all the British fighter squadrons into the Battle and that he had crippled the R.A.F. He ordered daylight bombing raids on British industrial centers.

On August 15 a hundred German bombers escorted by forty fighters struck at Tyneside, while more than eight hundred other Luftwaffe aircraft flew to the south of England to pin down British fighter strength.

It was the biggest struggle so far. Five major aerial battles were fought on a front of five hundred miles. All of Britain's twenty-two squadrons in the south were engaged, many of them two or three times. In all, German losses were seventy-six planes to thirty-four British.

"The next morning Londoners would calmly pick their way through the dust and rubble to carry on the struggle."

In that single August week the enemy lost 256 planes to the British 130.

It was a disaster for the Luftwaffe.

But Marshal Hermann Goering kept on. From his luxurious country home, Karin Hall, the man whom professional German officers contemptuously called "the fat boy" went from costly mistake to calamitous blunder. Having failed to finish the job of ruining British fighter power, he did not follow through in his attack on Britain's industry. He had already lost sight of his mission—to pave the way for invasion—as he turned to his dream of winning the war from the air. Now he decided that he would do this by terror. He would paralyze the heart of England.

Goering ordered the blitz on London.

It began on September 7, just a week before an Italian army invaded Egypt in an attempt to drive the British out of Africa. Many of those Tommies who stopped the Italians at Sidi Barrani heard of the horror of the London blitz and thanked their stars they were "safe at the front."

For two solid months London felt the full fury of the Luftwaffe. The Germans attacked by day and by night. Sometimes there were as many as 320 bombers escorted by six hundred fighters. At other times there were only a half-dozen or so, or even a lone wolf flashing down to drop his bombs and keep Londoners unnerved.

But London lost neither its nerve nor its sense of humor. The Luftwaffe might smash whole sections of the city, leaving only a few stark walls or chimneys standing to testify to the existence of an office block. But next morning Londoners would calmly pick their way through the dust and rubble to carry on the struggle. The Luftwaffe bombed Monkey Hill in the zoo, and newspapers carried reports that "the morale of the monkeys remained unaffected." The Luftwaffe stepped up daylight bombing, and cricket players complained that it was interfering with their game.

People were buried alive when entire buildings collapsed upon them in a splintering crash. But soldiers calmly dug them out even as the fury of fresh air raids fell upon them. Incendiary raids set fires by the thousand, and some raged on for days, but all were finally brought under control. Then Germans began dropping delayed-action bombs. These buried themselves in the ground and exploded later. They were a fearful weapon, for large groups of people might gather innocently over an "unexploded bomb," or UXB, only to have it explode in their faces.

Special UXB Squads were formed to uncover and disarm the delayed-action bombs. It took iron nerves to carry out such work. One famous UXB Squad was formed by the Earl of Suffolk, his female private secretary, and his aged chauffeur. They called themselves the "Holy Trinity." Smiling, chatting lightly to each other, the three disposed of thirty-four UXBs. Then the thirty-fifth went up with a roar, killing the Earl of Suffolk.

Such was the character of the people of London in the face of Marshal Goering's systematic terror. Eventually the Battle of Britain was to become a British victory. But it did not entirely end, of course, with those first few flaming months. Until the end of the war, London stood beneath the threat of attack from the air. But the great blaze of aerial battle that marked the period between July 10th and October 31st, 1940, ended in disastrous defeat for the Luftwaffe.

Germany lost 1,733 planes to 915 for Britain. Goering's golden dream became a black nightmare. Most of the credit for this shining victory belonged to that bold band of R.A.F. pilots who never stopped slashing at the invader. All of Britain was grateful to them. As Churchill said: "Never in the field of human conflict was so much owed by so many to so few."

Adolf Hitler, who had already sullenly postponed Operation Sea Lion, was forced to postpone it again until the spring of 1941. Even the Fuehrer realized that this was an empty gesture. By that time, it would not be possible to invade England.

But never mind, by that time the Battle of the Atlantic—raging again as never before—would have starved the British into submission. Or so Hitler thought.

10 | War beneath the Waves

"The only thing that ever really frightened me during the war," said Winston Churchill, "was the U-boat peril."

In World I the German submarines operated out of a few North Sea bases. But the Nazis, after the fall of France, held a coastline that ran from the Arctic to the Spanish coast. U-boats sailing from such French ports as Brest, Lorient, and St. Nazaire had double their old cruising radius. And the British had lost forever the hope of any assistance from the French navy in the Atlantic and Mediterranean.

A masterful, deadly hand was now at the German U-boat helm. It belonged to Rear Admiral Karl Doenitz, a daring and ruthless officer who had commanded a U-boat in World War I. He did not hesitate to tell his captains to shoot helpless sailors in the water to keep them from shipping out again.

Hitler admired Doenitz, and because of his standing with the Fuehrer, Doenitz had almost a free hand in running the U-boat war. He obtained the big new submarines he demanded, and sent them out into the North and South Atlantic in fanwise groups of eight to twenty.

These were the dreaded "wolfpacks."

From his headquarters in Lorient, "Papa" Doenitz knew where every one of his U-boats was. The moment one of them contacted a convoy, a report was radioed to Doenitz. While the contacting submarine shadowed the convoy, Doenitz sent in all the others in the area.

The wolves gathered at night. They rose silently to the surface, some of them even slipping in among the sheeplike convoys. Then they fired their torpedoes and dived below the surface. Half an hour later, they would surface again and renew the attack. It would go on all night, and sometimes through the day, from beneath the surface.

Allied losses became staggering. These were chiefly British, of course, although the Norwegian merchant fleet, fourth

Trainees at a German submarine school are receiving instruction aboard their U-boats.

Admiral Karl Doenitz conducts an inspection of coastal strong points.

largest in the world, had escaped Hitler and was serving the Allied cause.

Before France fell, 1,201,535 tons of cargo a week—exclusive of oil—had been brought to Britain by sea. A month later the wolfpacks cut this weekly average to 750,000 tons. In two more months, sinkings were much worse than they had ever been in the First World War. In October, 1940, the U-boats caught an Atlantic convoy of thirty-four ships and sank twenty of them. By January of 1941 the entrance of ships into British ports was *less than half* of what it had been a year earlier. In three months of 1941 the wolfpacks massacred 142 ships.

Britain was being strangled.

To her side, as of old, came her great and powerful neighbor from across the sea. Franklin Roosevelt, who had been reëlected to a record-breaking third term as president in November of 1940, put into effect his famous "short-of-war" policy of aid to England.

Because the United States feared Japanese ambitions in the Pacific as well as a Nazi conquest of Britain, she had already begun building a two-ocean navy during the summer of 1940. All sorts of weapons were being turned out in factories working around the clock.

But Britain had lost so much already she could not afford to buy all the weapons she needed. So President Roosevelt invented "Lend-Lease." He received from Congress the power to lend or lease any war material to any government "whose defense the President deems vital to the defense of the United States." The President explained: "Sup-

pose my neighbor's house catches fire and I have a length of garden hose four or five hundred feet away. If he can take my garden hose and connect it up with his hydrant, I may help him put out the fire. Now . . . I don't say to him before that operation, 'Neighbor, my hose cost me fifteen dollars; you have to pay me fifteen dollars for it.' No! . . . I don't want fifteen dollars—I want my garden hose back after the fire is over."

Most Americans approved of Lend-Lease, but many others did not. These were the isolationists, who still believed that America could stay out of the war. They did not understand that, if Hitler conquered England, there would soon be Nazi governments in South America and in the French West Indies right off American shores. The United States would really be "isolated" then—in the middle of a Nazi sea.

Already the United States had sent fifty old destroyers to Britain in return for the right to lease bases in Bermuda, Newfoundland, and the British West Indies. These destroyers had been quickly placed in convoy service, for it

President Roosevelt signing the historic Lend-Lease Act on March 11, 1941.

During a U-boat chase British Commander Frederic Walker shouts encouragement to one of the sloops in his patrol.

was obvious that the only way to counter the wolfpacks was to increase convoy protection. Better tactics were needed and better detection devices.

One good service used in the Battle of the Atlantic was sonar, or asdic as the British called it. It was housed in a steel bubble under the ship's hull. Sonar operators listened for a U-boat's propellers or sent out echo-ranging "pings" which the U-boat's hull returned. From these they could determine the enemy boat's location. In defense the Germans invented *Pillenwerfer*. This device shot out small gas bubbles which returned an echo "ping" similar to that returned by a ship's hull. It confused sonar operators.

Then there was radar. Although radar could not find a submerged ship, it could find the surfaced ones. "Huff-duff" — a high-frequency direction finder — picked up U-boat messages to other U-boats or to Doenitz. Through "huff-duff" a bearing could be taken on the U-boats. This information was of great help to convoys. Later, it would enable Allied

aircraft to surprise surfaced submarines, sometimes catching them idling while the crews were sunning themselves.

One successful U-boat fighting tactic was developed by Commander Frederic J. Walker of the Royal Navy. A tall, lean, driving man who had been at sea since he was seventeen, Walker invented "Operation Buttercup"—taken from his wife's nickname.

If the wolfpack launched a surface night attack, Walker's escort group would light the darkness with searchlights, rockets, and star shells. The U-boats would be forced to dive. Submerged, they would have to move slowly, giving Walker's ships a chance to plaster the whole area with a blanket of depth charges.

While escorting one convoy from Britain to Gibraltar, Walker's group sank three U-boats in a running battle. A fourth was damaged and forced to surface. But the German submarine was so close that Walker's guns could not be brought low enough to shoot at it. Walker put the helm of his ship hard over. He rammed the German U-boat just in front of the conning tower, blasting it with depth charges as it was going down.

Eventually the tactics born in Operation Buttercup were adopted by the Royal Navy. The United States Navy also adopted them after entering the "war short of war."

In April of 1941 President Roosevelt drew a line on a map of the Atlantic Ocean, dividing it in half along meridian 26 west. West of this line, he said, the United States Navy would defend American ships. United States patrols went right up to the new frontier, which was later extended to include Iceland, the stepping stone to Britain. At the invitation of the Icelandic government, the First Marine Brigade was sent to defend Iceland.

Now the German U-boats and American patrol craft were actually fighting one another. But Hitler closed his eyes to the American "war short of war." Much as he despised America, he did not want to bring the sleeping giant fully awake.

The Fuehrer kept his eyes shut because he thought he was winning the Battle of the Atlantic. At least it seemed that way. German surface warships had joined the fray.

The mighty battleship *Bismarck,* pride of the German navy, had broken free from her hiding place in Norway. Accompanied by the big *Prinz Eugen* and several smaller German warships, *Bismarck* met the giant British battle cruiser *Hood* off the coast of Greenland. There a battle was joined. One of *Bismarck's* opening salvos sent a shell crashing through *Hood's* lightly armored powder magazine. The great ship blew up. Then *Bismarck* also challenged the British battleship *Prince of Wales* and inflicted damage on her.

Assisted by destroyers and the cruisers *Suffolk* and *Norfolk,* the *Prince of Wales* pressed the attack. *Bismarck* and her escorts turned away, vanishing into the Arctic mists. There followed an exciting sea chase of some 1,750 miles before the *Bismarck* was finally caught off the French coast. Torpedo bombers from the carrier *Ark Royal* flew to the attack. They left the great dreadnought wallowing out of control, a sitting duck for British warships converging on her from all directions. A long time dying, the *Bismarck* sank to the bottom on May 27.

And so the Battle of the Atlantic raged on through the summer of 1941.

A direct hit blasts the 42,800-ton Bismarck *shortly before her sinking in the Atlantic.*

11 | The Balkans Bow

All through early 1941 Adolf Hitler had been secretly getting ready for an invasion of Russia.

He had done this partly by making sure of his southern flank, which rested in the lands known as the Balkans. Hungary and Rumania had already joined the Axis. But Hitler also needed Bulgaria and Yugoslavia. He had planned to have them under his control by the end of March, 1941.

In the meantime, Mussolini was to take care of the Mediterranean.

To the boastful Il Duce, this looked easy. The fall of France had put the French navy out of the war and left the Italian navy supreme in the Mediterranean. Still fancying himself a modern Caesar, Mussolini began speaking of the Mediterranean Sea as *mare nostrum,* Latin for "our sea."

There was some reason for this boast. Along the Mediterranean's southern shores all the lands except British-controlled Egypt were French or Italian. The French colonies were run by the pro-German Vichy Government. And on September 14, 1940, Mussolini had sent his armies plunging from Libya into Egypt, hoping to drive the British from that area.

On the northern fringe of the Mediterranean only neutral Spain and Greece were not Axis-dominated. Mussolini now decided to conquer Greece. He was jealous of Hitler's glory. And

he was annoyed because the Fuehrer had invaded France without telling him beforehand. Il Duce decided to do the same in Greece.

On October 28, 1940, the Italian army in Albania crossed the Greek frontier. There they received a reception rougher than the Finns had given the first Russian offensive. Superb mountain fighters, the Greeks quickly dealt the invaders a bloody repulse. Then they counterattacked. They not only threw the Italians out of Greece, they pursued them into Albania. Sixteen Greek divisions chased twenty-seven of Il Duce's for thirty miles beyond the frontier, and then kept them hemmed up in the Albanian mountains for months.

Mussolini was red-faced.

He became more so after the British Royal Navy struck a daring blow in the Mediterranean. A few weeks after the Greek invasion, airplanes from the British carrier *Illustrious* caught the Italian battle fleet in the harbor at Taranto. They put it out of action for six months.

A month later Mussolini received another rebuff in Africa, where he had been attempting without much success to drive the British from Egypt. If the Axis nations held Egypt, they would hold the Suez Canal. And with the Canal went the possibility of a hookup with a third partner, Japan, in the Far

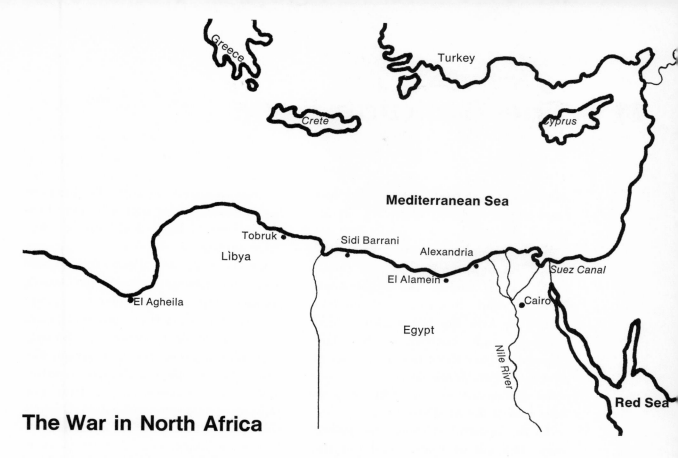

Greece

Turkey

Crete

Cyprus

Mediterranean Sea

Tobruk

Sidi Barrani

Alexandria

Libya

El Alamein

Suez Canal

El Agheila

Cairo

Egypt

Nile River

Red Sea

The War in North Africa

East. Also, the oil-rich lands of the Moslem world would come under Axis influence, and Turkey would probably enter the war on the Axis side.

But the Italian army, which Il Duce loved to compare to the invincible Roman legions of old, failed to penetrate very far into Egypt. They had halted at Sidi Barrani, just inside the frontier.

In the meantime, the Army of the Nile under General Sir Archibald Wavell had been strengthened. General Wavell received some big new Matilda tanks, and picked units of New Zealand, Australian, Polish, Indian, and Free French troops. In December Wavell attacked. His men drove through the back-pedaling Italians like a knife through butter. The jaunty Australians swept into battle singing "We're off to See

the Wizard."

The "Desert Gallop" had begun. It was a pell-mell retreat and pursuit. Matilda tanks clanked forward over the soft desert sands. A high-hearted young British armored officer sent back the message: "Have reached the second B in Buq Buq." Then Wavell's troops swept over the border into Libya, part of the Italian Kingdom. They took thousands of prisoners en route. By mid-January, 1941, the important coastal citadel of Tobruk had fallen to General Wavell. At a cost of less than 2,000 casualties and less than 500 dead, the Army of the Nile ruined ten Italian divisions and took 113,000 prisoners.

Next the British turned south to drive Italy out of Ethiopia.

Finally, they answered the Greek appeal for help. Some 57,000 soldiers,

59

On the African desert outside Bardia, Field Marshal Sir Archibald Wavell (right) confers with Lt. Gen. O'Connor.

mostly Anzacs (that is, Australians and New Zealanders), were detached from the Army of the Nile and shipped to Greece. On March 27 the Italian navy tried to intercept their convoy. Firing in the dark by radar, British warships sank three Italian cruisers and three destroyers. An Italian battleship was also severely damaged. The British lost two aircraft.

Hitler was enraged. He felt as if his partner hung around his neck like a millstone. Mussolini was fast losing control of the Mediterranean, and he had been defeated in Greece, Ethiopia, and North Africa. To rescue the situation, the Fuehrer sent General Erwin Rommel, with a mechanized division and an air force, to command the Axis forces in North Africa.

This was the famous general who was to earn the name of "Desert Fox." He was one of the German officers whom the Allies most respected. Handsome, dashing, Rommel had nearly trapped the British at Dunkirk, and in North Africa he was to torment them to death with his *Afrika Korps.*

On April 3, 1941, Rommel launched his offensive from Libya. In a series of lightning thrusts he forced Wavell to

Australian troops advance into Bardia behind a tank.

pull back to his bases in Egypt. Only Tobruk in Libya refused to fall. It was defended by those immortal "Rats of Tobruk," the gallant Australians who held out for eight months in Rommel's rear until they were finally relieved.

But Libya was once again in Axis hands, and with Rommel on the scene the Suez Canal was threatened as never before.

Now Hitler could turn to Greece— and also to Yugoslavia, where the fires of rebellion were burning. The warlike Yugoslavs were not nearly so tame as their leaders. Two days after the Yugoslav government had accepted Hitler's demands, a group of army officers rose in revolt.

On April 6, 1941, Hitler hurled the blitz into Yugoslavia and Greece.

The Yugoslavs were able to hold out only eleven days. A German army of 650,000 men, spearheaded by a thousand planes, rolled over the little Yugoslav revolutionary force like a steamroller. The mountainous terrain had proved no obstacle to the swift-moving panzer troops. Even so, thousands of ardent Yugoslavs melted into the mountains, from there to carry on a guerrilla warfare that kept many Nazi divisions engaged until the end of the war.

Still farther south, a Nazi army of half a million men was rolling through the combined Greco-British defenses. Here, too, it was only a matter of time. The blitz was working with the pulverizing thoroughness of old. Finally the Greek government informed its British allies: "You have done your best to save us. We are finished. But the war is

General Erwin Rommel, "The Desert Fox" (third from left), consults with his staff in the field.

not yet lost. Save as much as you can of your army to help win elsewhere."

The British force of 57,000 men was now down to 43,000. They fell back, fighting dogged rear-guard actions. On April 23 they had reached the southern beaches of Greece. A smaller Dunkirk was in the offing. Fortunately the next few nights were moonless. Hiding out from the Luftwaffe by day, smashing their equipment and drowning their tanks by night, the Anzacs awaited evacuation. Rescue craft arrived on the last night in April. Half of the men were taken back to Egypt, and the other half were sent to the island of Crete.

But Crete was next on Hitler's list. The Axis needed this vital base off the Greek coast. It had an excellent harbor used by the British Royal Navy. It had airfields from which the British could protect the lifeline through the Suez or attack the Italian navy.

Crete was to be the scene of the first full-scale airborne assault of the war. At eight o'clock in the morning of May 20, 1941, German airplanes fell upon Crete

Floating down from the sky, Nazi para-troopers join the battle on Crete.

like clouds of fire-spitting hawks. They blasted roads and airfields and knocked out antiaircraft batteries.

Then came the paratroops.

They parachuted from transports flying at heights of six hundred or three hundred feet. Among them was the famous Max Schmeling, former heavy-

weight champion of the world. Many of them wore camouflage uniforms. Others had on New Zealand battle dress to confuse the Allied soldiers. Some of these paratroops floating down from the skies also turned out to be dummies designed to draw off British fire.

Next came the gliders, towed by lumbering old transport planes. They were strung out ten or eleven in a line. Cut free from their mother plane, they glided down in belly landings. Instantly their doors were flung open, and men sprang to the ground.

In a matter of minutes the Germans had landed 15,000 men equipped with rifles, light and heavy machine guns, artillery, and radio equipment.

But it also seemed, at first, that they had parachuted straight into hell. Crete's defenders had a duck shoot. They picked off the parachutists as they floated with slow helplessness toward earth. Few of the first 3,500 Germans who jumped survived. Many fell in the sea and were drowned. Others were caught in tree-tops and picked off at leisure. Leaderless bands were herded into rocky ravines and slaughtered.

But more and more kept coming in. German planes arrived by crash-landing on the airfield. A steady stream of reinforcements flowed into the battle, while the Luftwaffe pinned down all enemy vehicles. German planes also drove the British navy from Crete after the first day.

Gaining strength, the German invaders drove across the island. By the end of May, the fighting was all over.

Once more British warships came

under cover of darkness to take off a defeated force. Once more the British lion seemed to be slinking away, trailing his tail between his legs, while the Axis score mounted steadily higher.

Austria, Czechoslovakia, Rumania, Hungary, and Bulgaria had been added to the Nazi camp by brutal methods of "diplomacy." And poor Finland had been forced into war again—this time on Germany's side. Little Albania was in Italy's power. And dangling from Hitler's war belt were the scalps of Poland, Norway, Denmark, Luxembourg, Holland, Belgium, France, North Africa, Yugoslavia, Greece, and Crete. Where would the Fuehrer strike next?

In Russia.

Weary British troops rest by the roadside during the retreat in Greece.

12 | Hitler Turns on Russia

Historians have continued to ask: Why did Hitler attack Russia?

It was a foolish thing to do, especially with Britain still defiant. Hitler should have learned from the example of Napoleon. Although a greater military genius than Hitler, Napoleon had invaded Russia to his eventual ruin.

Hitler, however, imagined that he was superior to Napoleon. And he was determined to crush the Soviet Union. Russia would serve the German "master race" as a supplier of food and minerals and slave labor. As early as December, 1940, Hitler had ordered the Russian invasion to be worked out. The plan was called Operation Barbarossa.

"When Barbarossa commences the world will hold its breath!" Hitler said.

The world did gasp in surprise and dismay that day of June 22, 1941, when a force of 150 German divisions spearheaded by 2,700 airplanes crashed into Russia.

Premier Joseph Stalin had been warned by both President Roosevelt and Prime Minister Churchill that his Nazi ally would turn on him. But Stalin did not believe them. He had always hated the democracies. So the Soviet armies were caught completely by surprise.

All along a front of 1,800 miles the Russian defenses began to collapse. Within a week the Luftwaffe had knocked the Soviet air force from the skies. By July 2 the Germans had cap-

tured 150,000 Russian soldiers, 1,200 tanks and 600 big guns. Everyone recalled Russia's invasion of Finland. The Soviet army was rotten, they said. Stalin had ruined it by executing his best generals back in 1936. Few experts in either London or Washington believed that Russia could hold out until Christmas. Hitler's prediction that Russia would fall in six weeks began to look modest.

Eighteen days after the invasion began, the central German thrust had carried four hundred miles to Smolensk. Moscow was only two hundred miles away.

There was also great success in the northern drive on Leningrad.

In the south, German formations were racing toward Stalingrad. The people of the Ukraine, who had always hated being ruled by Moscow, flocked toward the German conquerors in thousands. They even cheered them on. With stupid brutality, the Germans killed many of them and enslaved the rest. Shocked, the Ukraine returned to the standard of the hammer and the sickle. But Hitler did not care.

"Russia is broken!" he shouted to the world. "She will never rise again."

Unknown to Hitler, the Russian bear was only temporarily stunned. Many factors were at work for Stalin. First, the very swiftness of the German successes had forced them to spread their formations thin. Soon the Russians were

In a typical blitzkrieg action, a Nazi unit takes over a Russian village.

striking at the flanks of these far-flung columns. Second, in his vanity Hitler had said there were to be no retreats. Prevented by the Fuehrer's order from withdrawing and regrouping, the German generals found it difficult to meet the stiffening Russian resistance. Third, Russia was soon to get help from the Allies. Stalin was not ashamed to call for it, even demand it, *immediately*. And Mr. Churchill said in a broadcast: "Any man or state who fights against Nazism will have our aid." Fourth, the "scorched earth" policy proclaimed by Stalin slowed up the German advance.

Nothing was to be left for the invaders. Houses were burned; cattle were slaughtered and eaten; roads were wrecked and power plants blown up; crops were plowed under and factories dismantled.

By autumn, though stuffed with glory, the Wehrmacht had to slow down to regroup for the final lunge to Moscow. This began on October 2.

"Today begins the decisive battle of the year," Hitler told his armies.

They sprang forward again from their bases four hundred miles inside Russia. In three weeks they were within seventy miles of the capital. Then the attack bogged down. Hitler's generals argued

German soldiers are put to work in an attempt to stop fires ignited by the retreating Russians.

that it should be called off and renewed in the spring. The Russian winter was falling early. "No!" Hitler thundered.

The offensive was renewed. All during November of 1941 the troops ground slowly toward Moscow. Snow, fog, and rain engulfed them in a cold sea of misery. Temperatures were dropping rapidly. But they struggled on.

December 2, 1941. They were in the suburbs of Moscow. They could see the gilded towers of the Kremlin.

The thermometer fell to zero.

Equipped with light clothing, accustomed to nothing like the bitter Russian winter, the German soldiers suffered torments. Weapons froze, food froze, flesh froze. Tankmen and truckers had to run their engines every few hours lest they freeze and burst. Sometimes they had to build fires beneath them. Rations were slow in coming to the front. Soon the German soldiers were eating frozen horses to stay alive.

The Russians, on the other hand, were equipped for winter. They could live in it. And while front-line troops held the freezing Germans at arm's length, a huge reserve of troops and tanks was being built up to the rear. When this force was ready, Marshal Georgi Zhukov sent it surging forward against the Germans.

Hitler's divisions were caught with their tanks and trucks frozen in the snow. They were driven back. Eventually, the Russian offensive would send the Germans reeling back a distance of two hundred miles. Hitler's losses in five months of furious fighting would total nearly 800,000 casualties, and he would never get so close to Moscow again.

December 6, 1941—that was the day Zhukov launched his counterattack; that was the date the Russian bear turned on his tormentor.

The next day, as all the world knows, Japan awoke the sleeping American giant.

Soviet army machine gunners fire on enemy submachine gunners hidden in houses.

General Tojo was now the premier of Japan. Tojo's plan was to put half the population of the world under Japanese control. Emperor Hirohito would rule the entire Far East.

To accomplish his goal Tojo planned to destroy the United States Pacific Fleet, based at Pearl Harbor in Hawaii. After that he would knock out British and American air power in Malaya and the Philippines. Then the islands of the Pacific and all of Southeast Asia would fall to Japan. Nippon—the ancient name for Japan—would be free to complete the conquest of China, which she had first invaded in 1931.

All of this conquering and looting would be done behind a line of island outposts and the fighting ships and airplanes of the mighty Japanese navy. By the time America recovered from the loss of her Pacific Fleet, this line would be too strong to be broken. America would quickly tire of battering at it and would be ready to talk peace, Tojo thought. He scorned Americans as soft lovers of luxury. After a few bloody battles they would be eager to let Japan keep her stolen treasure. And the British would be so hard pressed by Hitler that they would have little to spare for the Far East.

That was Tojo's war plan. He got the chance to put it into effect in late 1941 after America began protesting against Japan's continued presence in China.

Tojo sent a special representative to Washington to help the Japanese ambassador negotiate. They were to try to get the United States to agree to Japan's presence in China but, even if they were not successful Tojo figured that they would be keeping the Americans occupied while the sneak attack on Pearl Harbor was launched.

A sneak attack was an old Japanese trick. It had been used to destroy the Russian fleet in 1904. The new version had been planned by Fleet Admiral Isoroku Yamamoto. He collected Japan's six newest and largest aircraft carriers, carrying a total of 423 combat planes.

Japanese Premier Hideki Tojo.

And he gathered a support force of two battleships, two cruisers and ten or eleven smaller ships. This striking force was placed under the command of Vice Admiral Chuichi Nagumo.

To escape attention, Nagumo's ships stole out of the Inland Sea in twos and threes. They met again in lonely Tankan Bay in the Kurile Islands north of Japan. On November 26 they set sail for Pearl Harbor.

Nagumo chose a route through rough waters rarely sailed by commercial ships. He ordered his captains to sink any unfriendly ship that might discover them. They saw none, not even an enemy aircraft. But it was a foul voyage. Mountainous black waves buffeted Nagumo's vessels. Many men were washed overboard. Still the force bored on, while Nagumo anxiously awaited word from Yamamoto. War might still be averted and the striking force recalled.

But from Washington came the diplomats' report that President Roosevelt would not agree to Japan's remaining in China.

This meant war.

Tojo instructed the diplomats to present the Japanese declaration of war at one o'clock Sunday afternoon December 7, 1941. At exactly that moment—7:30 A.M. Honolulu time—the Emperor's "glorious young eagles" would be pouncing on the unsuspecting American warships. This was treachery unrivaled in modern history.

Out in the fogs and mists of the North Pacific, Admiral Nagumo read the message from Admiral Yamamoto. It said:

"Climb Mount Niitake."

In the Japanese code that meant, "Attack!"

Nagumo turned his carriers south and sent them plunging through mounting seas to Hawaii.

At Pearl Harbor that fateful Sunday morning there were eight battleships moored neatly along Battleship Row. They were *Nevada, Arizona, Tennessee, West Virginia, Maryland, Oklahoma, California,* and *Pennsylvania.* With them were five cruisers and twenty-six destroyers and other craft.

Luckily for America, the Fleet's three aircraft carriers plus seven cruisers were in the open seas.

About one-third of the Pearl Harbor crews were on shore leave. Many officers were also ashore. Antiaircraft batteries were only partially manned. Most of the ammunition was in padlocked steel chests. As the hour of the Japanese attack neared, some of the ships had piped their crews below for breakfast. Others were busy at the morning flag raising.

Two Army radar operators, one still in the training stage, did notice a huge number of blips on their warning screen. They notified a rather uninterested young officer, who told them it was probably a flight of American B-17s arriving from California.

No American patrol craft were searching the skies that lovely morning. Even worse, all American aircraft in the vicinity were out on the fields in plain view. They were lined up wing to wing, because the Pearl Harbor commanders feared sabotage more than direct Japanese attack. These commanders had been alerted to the possibility of war with Japan. But they thought the crisis had passed a week before.

In Washington, the secret of the Japanese plan was guessed when it was observed that, though one o'clock of a Sunday afternoon was an odd hour to deliver a diplomatic note, the time in Hawaii would be just 7:30 A.M. And early morning would be just the right time to launch a surprise attack from aircraft carriers!

General George C. Marshall was called. General Marshall was chief of staff of the United States Army and also chairman of the joint chiefs of staff. Thus he was America's number one officer next to the President. General Marshall sent a warning to Pearl Harbor. But it went as a commercial telegram! It wasn't delivered until after the Japanese naval fliers had done their worst.

Not even the sinking of a Japanese midget submarine outside the harbor early that morning had alerted the Americans. They still thought themselves at peace. Church bells were ringing when, at five minutes before eight, Battleship Row suddenly became ablaze with fire and thunder.

Forty Japanese torpedo bombers and fifty-one dive bombers, accompanied by about fifty high-level bombers and fifty fighters, swooped in for the first attack. The torpedo bombers or "Kates" came skimming low over the water to release their fish. The dive-bombing Vals plummeted straight down, dropping bombs and 16-inch armor-piercing shells which penetrated steel decks and exploded below.

Oklahoma hadn't a chance. Three torpedos tore her open like giant can openers. She began rolling over. There wasn't time to counterflood and right her, even to fight from her. Men crawled over her exposed starboard side as she kept on rolling. Two more torpedoes struck her. She turned over and showed the bright blue Pacific sky her keel.

Many of *Oklahoma's* survivors climbed aboard *Maryland,* moored alongside the stricken ship. They helped the *Maryland* crew to fight back. For the Americans were no longer stunned. They knew the identity, now, of the strange planes that had suddenly begun diving, darting, and flashing among them. They recognized the red-ball insignias painted on the wings, and the grinning faces in the cockpits. Even as Battleship Row rocked and roared and smoked like a battle arena of the gods, American sailors and Marines were battering padlocks off the ready chests with ringing blows of axes and mauls. They were passing out the ammunition and fighting back. Men on shore leave were racing back to the docks, jumping into small craft and churning out to their ships. Some of them were swimming back.

Already the stupefying message had been flashed to the United States:

AIR RAID, PEARL HARBOR—THIS IS NO DRILL.

The *Maryland* fought on. Protected from torpedoes by the hull of *Oklahoma,* she escaped with only two bomb hits and would be the first to sail to sea in revenge.

Tennessee and *West Virginia,* also moored together, suffered the fate of

Oklahoma and *Maryland. West Virginia* on the outboard side was hit by two bombs and six or seven torpedoes. She began listing. Counterflooding was ordered. *West Virginia* straightened and sank upright. *Tennessee,* protected from torpedoes, was racked by bomb hits and fires started by flaming debris from *Arizona* moored behind her.

The repair ship with which *Arizona* was moored did not protect this doomed battlewagon. She was torn apart by bombs and torpedoes. She sank so fast that hundreds of sailors were trapped below.

California, moored alone, also went down. Two torpedoes tore her open, and a bomb which exploded her magazine gave her the death blow. *Nevada,* also alone, was the only battleship to get under way. At the time of the surprise attack, *Nevada's* color guard was raising the flag while her band played "The Star-Spangled Banner." A skimming Kate, which had just torpedoed *Arizona,* roared overhead. Her rear gunner began strafing. No one moved. The flag, torn by a bullet, was raised. A second Kate made for the band, strafing viciously. But the anthem was finished without pause. Then *Nevada's* guns began blasting. One, perhaps two, torpedo bombers were hit. The Kates kept clear of *Nevada.* Nevertheless the great old ship was staggered by a torpedo. She got under way, standing bravely down the ship channel, straddled by near misses and obscured by smoke. Eventually she slid aground.

Pennsylvania, luckiest of the battleships, was safely in dry dock, out of torpedo reach. She took only one severe bomb hit, and put up such a fierce umbrella of ack-ack that most of the enemy planes gave her a wide berth.

Meanwhile, all over the principal Hawaiian island of Oahu, American air power was being systematically destroyed. Everywhere the Japanese high-level bombers and strafing fighter planes caught the American aircraft parked wing to wing. Only a few American planes rose into the skies to challenge the men of Nippon.

A second wave of planes was still to strike at Pearl Harbor and Oahu, but most of the damage was done by the first.

By the morning of December 8, seven of the Pacific Fleet's eight battleships were sunk or very badly damaged, and half the base's aircraft were destroyed.

In Washington, Secretary of State Cordell Hull heard of the attack while the Japanese diplomats awaited him in his drawing room. They came into his office and handed him their declaration. It was a document filled with insulting charges against America. Hull read it. Choking with rage, he said: "I have never seen a document that was more crowded with infamous falsehoods and distortions—infamous falsehoods and distortions on a scale so huge that I never imagined that any government on this planet was capable of uttering them."

The Japanese left without a word.

In the Pacific, Admiral Nagumo and his glorious young eagles sailed homeward in triumph.

The United States was now at war.

Only the keel of the capsized Oklahoma *remains above water, but alongside the stricken vessel the men on the* Maryland *begin to fight back.*

Planes burn on a littered airfield after attacks by Japanese dive bombers.

14 | The Japanese Victory Flood

The Japanese attack on Pearl Harbor united the American people as never before. Once the first shock had worn off, a low growl of anger rose from the nation. Never had the American people experienced such treachery.

The following day President Roosevelt spoke to both houses of Congress, beginning his speech with: "Yesterday, December 7, 1941—a date which will live in infamy . . ." Afterward Congress declared war on Japan without debate and with only a single dissenting vote.

All over the country, recruiting offices were jammed with young men volunteering to fight the Japanese. They slept in the corridors awaiting their turn for physical examinations.

In Germany, Adolf Hitler was jubilant to hear that American naval power had been crippled. He had no way of knowing that all but one of the seven stricken battleships would be back in action within a year, and that none of the Pacific Fleet's three carriers had been harmed. Hitler declared war on America, too, and Mussolini followed suit. Britain had already declared war on Japan, and the United States was quick to declare war on Germany and Italy. Soon Latin America came to the Allies' side.

Within a week thirty-five nations, rep-

Declaring Japan guilty of an "unprovoked and dastardly" attack, President Roosevelt asks Congress for a declaration of war.

resenting half the population of the world, were engaged in this greatest of wars. In fact, the war was now so vast that not even the unengaged half of the world's population would escape its effects.

Confident of victory, President Roosevelt told the nation: "We are going to win the war and we are going to win the peace that follows."

But even as he spoke, the outlook for the Allies grew darker.

In the Philippines, American air power was destroyed on the ground. This was a terrible blow to General Douglas MacArthur, the American commander there. He had depended on using the big Flying Fortress bombers to hold off Japanese power until the Navy could come to his aid. Even with the Navy temporarily crippled, he could have hurled the Flying Fortresses at the approaching Japanese invasion fleet.

But now most of them were gone, and on December 10 the Japanese made the first of six amphibious or waterborne landings on the big northern island of Luzon. The roll call of Allied disaster began to mount, as the Japanese captured the United States island of Guam, landed in Thailand, landed in Malaya to the rear of the big British bastion at Singapore, seized Hong Kong on the coast of China, and sank the British battleship *Prince of Wales* and battle cruiser *Repulse*. This last blow left the Japanese navy supreme in the Pacific. And on land, the Japanese seemed invincible.

Only at Wake Island did they suffer reverses. On December 11 the Marine garrison at Wake hurled back a Japanese invasion, and a thrill of hope ran through America at the news that a relief force was speeding toward the island. But the relief was recalled before it reached Wake. On December 23 the Japanese returned in greater strength and Wake finally fell.

Once again the Japanese timetable of conquest resumed its precise and irresistible march. Before the year of 1941 was finished, there were numerous additional landings in the Philippines and General MacArthur was in full retreat toward the peninsula of Bataan in southwestern Luzon. Manila, the capital of the Philippines, was evacuated.

The Japanese had almost absolute control of the air. The few remaining American bombers were soon expended, and the pitifully small United States Asiatic Fleet was all but driven from the surface of the sea by flashing, red-balled enemy aircraft. Try as it might, the United States Navy simply could not get reinforcements and supplies to the gallant Philippine garrison. There was no end of bravery in making the futile attempt. One of the first American heroes in World War II was the dashing bomber pilot Colin Kelly.

The day after most of General MacArthur's bombers were destroyed, Colin Kelly flew one of the few surviving Flying Fortresses out to intercept the Japanese invasion fleet. He saw a big ship below and dropped a string of six-hundred-pound bombs. One of them hit! Before the plane could get back to base, Japanese fighters attacked. Kelly's crew fought them off, but six more came

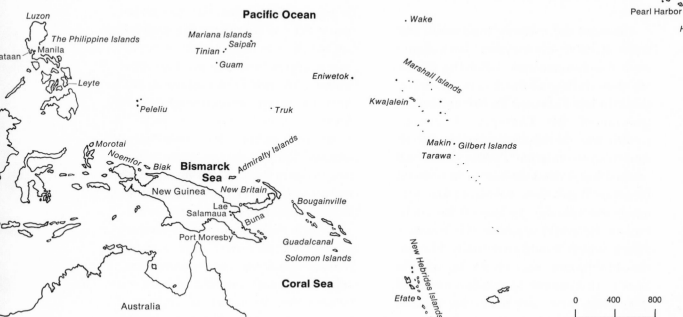

The Pacific Island Groups

China
Japan
Tokyo
Midway
Okinawa
Iwo Jima
Formosa
Pacific Ocean
Wake
Pearl Harbor
Hawaii
Luzon
Mariana Islands
The Philippine Islands
Saipan
Marshall Islands
Bataan
Tinian
Manila
Guam
Eniwetok
Kwajalein
Leyte
Peleliu
Truk
Makin · Gilbert Islands
Morotai
Tarawa
Noemfor · Biak
Bismarck Sea
Admiralty Islands
New Guinea · New Britain
Lae
Salamaua
Buna
Bougainville
Port Moresby
Guadalcanal
New Hebrides Islands
Solomon Islands
Efate
Coral Sea
Australia

0   400   800

roaring in. A crewman fell dead. The plane was rocked by shellfire, and aflame. "Bail out!" Colin Kelly ordered. The men jumped, but Kelly remained at the controls. He was killed before he could jump.

Although Colin Kelly had not sunk an enemy battleship as was at first believed, he had done something even more gallant. He had given up his life so that his comrades might live.

That was the spirit which held the Filipinos and Americans together on Bataan, and later in the murky tunnel beneath the rocky fortress island of Corregidor just off the tip of the peninsula. Even while Singapore was falling and the British were evacuating Malaya, the Filipinos and Americans held out on the Philippines. Ragged and red-eyed, bombed by day and shelled by night, living off the flesh of lizards, monkeys and snakes, they fought on and sang their sardonic song:

Captain Colin P. Kelly, Jr.

We're the Battling Bozos of Bataan:
No mama, no papa, no Uncle Sam,
No aunts, no uncles, no cousins, no
nieces,
No pills, no planes, or artillery pieces—

Although these lonely men could not know it, their countrymen back home were deeply concerned. But the Japanese were sinking all the American supply ships. In late February President Manuel Quezon of the Philippine Commonwealth was taken off Corregidor by an American submarine. Then, when all seemed lost, President Roosevelt ordered General MacArthur to leave. He was much too valuable to lose. If he could escape, he could organize the counterattack which would eventually liberate the Philippines and crush Japan. On March 12 General MacArthur boarded a torpedo boat and made his famous dash to Mindanao in the south. Flying on to Australia by bomber, he was greeted as a savior.

"I came through," he said, "and I shall return."

Back on Bataan the new commander, General Jonathan Wainwright, led his men in a magnificent stand lasting for another month. But by May 6 the Japanese were within yards of Malinta Tunnel, a network of underground passages on the island fortress of Corregidor. While his men were spiking guns, burning codes, and smashing equipment, General Wainwright composed his last sad message for President Roosevelt:

WITH BROKEN HEART AND HEAD BOWED IN SADNESS BUT NOT IN SHAME I REPORT TO YOUR EXCELLENCY THAT I MUST ARRANGE TERMS FOR THE SURRENDER OF THE FORTIFIED ISLANDS OF MANILA BAY. . . .

THERE IS A LIMIT OF HUMAN ENDURANCE AND THAT LIMIT HAS LONG SINCE BEEN PAST. WITHOUT PROSPECT OF RELIEF I FEEL IT IS MY DUTY TO MY COUNTRY AND TO MY GALLANT TROOPS TO END THIS USELESS EFFUSION OF BLOOD AND HUMAN SACRIFICE.

IF YOU AGREE, MR. PRESIDENT, PLEASE SAY TO THE NATION THAT MY TROOPS AND I HAVE ACCOMPLISHED ALL THAT IS HUMANLY POSSIBLE AND THAT WE HAVE UPHELD THE BEST TRADITIONS OF THE UNITED STATES AND ITS ARMY.

MAY GOD BLESS AND PRESERVE YOU AND GUIDE YOU AND THE NATION IN THE EFFORT TO ULTIMATE VICTORY.

WITH PROFOUND REGRET AND WITH CONTINUED PRIDE IN MY GALLANT TROOPS I GO TO MEET THE JAPANESE COMMANDER. GOOD-BYE, MR. PRESIDENT.

The roll call of Japanese conquest was complete: Pearl Harbor, Indochina,

General Douglas MacArthur in his head-quarters on Corregidor.

A captured Japanese war picture showing General Jonathan Wainwright as he broadcast the announcement of the surrender of Corregidor Island.

Thailand, Malaya, Hong Kong, Singapore, Burma, the Dutch East Indies, and now the Philippines. Not even Adolf Hitler could match the speed and the breadth of this marvelous march of victory. Australia was now in peril; great China was all but cut off from the world, and even India lay beneath the menace of that Rising Sun now so high in the Pacific.

But while the Allied world was plunged in gloom, there came the electrifying news of an amazing event: American airplanes had bombed Tokyo!

Until the end of the war, the Japanese could never unravel the mystery of how they had felt the whip of American air power at the very height of their own success.

The explanation is simple, The Navy had trained a force of Army Air Corps pilots to fly big bombers from plunging carrier decks. Sixteen of these B-25 Mitchells under Colonel James H. Doolittle sailed in a carrier force led by Admiral William F. ("Bull") Halsey. At a point 668 miles from Tokyo, they took off and dropped their bombs on the thunderstruck Japanese capital. Then, because they could not land on tiny carrier decks, they flew on to China or crashed in the ocean off her coast. Eight fliers and crewmen were caught by the Japanese, and three of them were executed after a mock trial.

Although this dramatic raid was not nearly the equal of the Pearl Harbor attack, it had the effect of boosting American morale. More, the stunned Japanese decided to keep many of their airplanes at home to protect Tokyo. Most important, they speeded up their timetable of conquest to an extent that put them on the road to ruin.

Midway: | 15
Japan Is Halted

After her astounding six months of triumph, Japan became over-confident. She overreached herself in deciding to push her island outposts closer to America. But by doing so she hoped she might even be able to conquer Australia.

In May, 1942, two Japanese invasion forces set out for Port Moresby in New Guinea and the Solomon Islands farther south. They were going to seize bases for airfields that would give Japan air mastery in the Coral Sea. The troop transports were protected by battleships and cruisers which would bombard the enemy before the invading forces landed. Also protecting them was a big striking force of carriers, which entered the Coral Sea to sweep it clear of Allied power.

The group bound for the Solomons met no difficulties. Japanese troops went ashore at tiny Tulagi Island.

But the group bound for New Guinea, sailing under the protection of the light carrier *Shoho*, was intercepted by pilots from the big American carriers *Lexington* and *Yorktown*. The Americans sank *Shoho* in ten minutes, a record for the war. *Lexington's* dive-bomber commander signaled jubilantly: "Scratch one flattop!"

As a result, the New Guinea group was forced to turn back.

But one day later Japanese pilots from the big carriers *Shokaku* and *Zuikaku* found the Americans. That was the undoing of poor old "Lady Lex," as the *Lexington* was called. Torn by torpedoes, battered by bombs, and listing, she was nevertheless headed home when a series of internal explosions gave her her death blows.

This series of naval actions is known as the Battle of the Coral Sea. The result slightly favored the Japanese: one light carrier lost to one big carrier. But two of the big Japanese flattops were so badly damaged that they were not able to join the next big air-sea fight, the very turning point of the Pacific War. And the Japanese had been turned away from Port Moresby.

Admiral Isoroku Yamamoto was in a hurry to destroy the remnant of the American Pacific Fleet before 1943. Otherwise, as he knew from his experience as a naval attaché in Washington, American industrial might would wipe out the naval edge Japan had gained at Pearl Harbor. So Yamamoto planned an operation which would force the Americans into a decisive sea battle. He decided to invade the Aleutian Islands in the North Pacific and Midway Island in the Central Pacific. If the Americans did not defend these islands, then Japan would have expanded her empire without effort. If the United States Navy did come out to fight, then Yamamoto would have the decisive battle he desired.

Collecting a powerful fleet of 162

ships, Yamamoto divided them into a large and a small force. The small one, sailing first, was to invade the Aleutians. Yamamoto hoped that the Americans would rush ships from the Midway area to the Aleutians. If they did they would weaken themselves in the area where he would be strongest. He would destroy them there at Midway, and then be able to overwhelm the others at his leisure. Even if the Americans did not take his northern bait, Yamamoto was still confident that he could annihilate them at Midway.

Against Yamamoto's 162 ships Admiral Chester W. Nimitz had only 76 ships. But Nimitz had the advantage of knowing enemy intentions. The Japanese secret code had been broken by American experts even before the Pearl Harbor attack. Thus enemy messages could be intercepted and deciphered.

Nimitz was not deceived by Yamamoto's feint in the north around the Aleutian Islands. He knew that Midway and his fleet were the enemy objectives. And he placed his carriers—*Yorktown, Hornet,* and *Enterprise*—northeast of Midway.

The Japanese, meanwhile, occupied the islands of Attu and Kiska in the Aleutians.

But the main strike was still to be directed at Midway, and Admiral Nagumo—the hero of Pearl Harbor—was selected to command it. He had in his fleet the big carriers *Akagi, Kaga, Hiryu,* and *Soryu,* all veterans of the Pearl Harbor attack.

Admiral Nagumo's combat planes were launched at Midway itself. They struck with savage fury, but the Americans fought desperately to save their installations. Midway's defense was so resolute that Admiral Nagumo decided he needed to hurl a second strike to knock out the island.

This is exactly what Rear Admiral Raymond A. Spruance, in command of *Enterprise* and *Hornet,* had calculated he would do. Spruance hoped to hit Nagumo's flattops while they were refueling and rearming for this second strike. This is when an aircraft carrier is most vulnerable, with bombs on deck and gasoline lines running.

On June 4 American patrol planes found the enemy carriers. They were sailing in boxlike formation over a sparkling blue sea, beneath a bright blue sky dotted with fleecy white clouds. Torpedo bombers, dive bombers, and fighters roared aloft from American carrier decks.

But Nagumo had changed his course, and the dive bombers and fighters from *Hornet* missed the enemy flattops. Her Devastator torpedo bombers did not. They attacked without fighter cover, and were slaughtered. It was the sad story of an inferior plane being methodically cut to bits. Every one of the fifteen attacking Devastators was shot down. When the *Enterprise's* torpedo squadron attacked, ten out of fourteen were sent plunging into the sea. *Yorktown* also lost all but four. It looked like an American disaster. The Japanese seemed to have won the Battle of Midway and, perhaps, the war.

But then the great Dauntless dive bombers from both carriers found the enemy. Revenge for Pearl Harbor was at hand!

Lieutenant Commander Clarence W. McClusky had two squadrons of Dauntlesses, thirty-seven in all. He himself took half of them down on the carrier *Kaga,* and Lieutenant W. E. Gallaher led the others at *Akagi.*

They stood on their noses at an altitude of 14,000 feet and came screaming down.

Akagi, with Admiral Nagumo aboard, was staggered by a bomb exploding in her hangar. Supplies of torpedoes began detonating like giant firecrackers. Another bomb fell among rearming planes on the flight deck. Flames engulfed the ship. Admiral Nagumo transferred his flag to the cruiser *Nagara. Akagi* was abandoned and sunk by a destroyer's torpedo.

Kaga also sank. Four bombs convulsed her and set her blazing from stem to stern. Then an internal explosion racked her, and she went down with a hiss.

Now *Yorktown's* Dauntlesses under Lieutenant Commander Maxwell F. Leslie had found *Soryu.* Sixteen of them pounced upon her as she was turning into the wind to launch planes. Three bombs struck her and she had to be abandoned. The United States submarine *Nautilus* finished off *Soryu* with a torpedo.

Nagumo had one big carrier left— *Hiryu.* He ordered her attack groups off to fall on *Yorktown.* Most of the forty Japanese planes were shot down. But three dive-bombing Vals scored three bomb hits. Then a quartet of low-flying Kates got two torpedoes into the American carrier, and the order "Abandon Ship" was broadcast. Still afloat twenty-four hours later, but unable to defend herself, *Yorktown* was put on the bottom by an enemy submarine's torpedo.

The Americans struck back.

Hiryu was brought under attack even at the moment the enemy aviators were striking at *Yorktown.* Lieutenant Gallaher led twenty-four Dauntlesses down on the Japanese ship. Four solid bomb hits put the last of the veteran carriers on the ocean floor not far from the scene of their infamous triumph at Pearl Harbor.

Admiral Yamamoto called off his attack and sailed home. He had lost his entire fast carrier group, the big sluggers of modern naval warfare. All the way home the despairing Yamamoto kept close to his cabin. For the first time in history the Japanese navy had been beaten. Thereafter Imperial Headquarters ordered that the word "Midway" was never to be mentioned.

For the Japanese military now knew that they had reached the high-water mark of their success. From the Battle of Midway on, they were on the defensive. And the tide now turning against them was to roll them still farther back at a little-known island with a coastline as long as its name.

Guadalcanal.

Aboard the damaged Yorktown *crew members work desperately to save their ship.*

16 | Guadalcanal: The Tide Turns

Tiny little Tulagi, which the Japanese had occupied on May 3, 1942, was one of the smallest of the Solomon Islands—just big enough for a seaplane base.

But about fifteen miles across the channel was the big and beautiful island of Guadalcanal. A mile inland from Guadalcanal's white beaches and gently nodding coconut palms were wide and level fields of kunai grass. These were ideal for airplane runways, and the Japanese soon began building an airfield there.

Hearing of this, United States military leaders reacted swiftly. The importance of Guadalcanal as an air base was recognized by Admiral Ernest J. King, commander in chief of the United States Fleet. From Guadalcanal enemy airplanes could bomb the supply ships coming over the American lifeline to Australia. But if America took Guadalcanal, she would be opening the front gate on the road back to the Philippines.

Admiral King consulted with General Marshall, after which a message was sent to Vice Admiral Robert Ghormley in New Zealand. It instructed him to occupy and defend Tulagi and adjacent positions—Guadalcanal and other islands in the Southern Solomons—in order to deny these areas to the enemy and to provide the United States with bases in preparation for further offensive action.

Admiral Ghormley immediately showed the message to a strong-jawed, soft-spoken Marine major general named Alexander A. Vandegrift. General Vandegrift was astounded. His own First Marine Division was to make the assault, and it would be launched the first week of August. That gave him little more than a month to prepare. At the moment his division was strung out in ships ranging from California to New Zealand. When the regiments arrived, they were expecting to undergo months of training. Although Vandegrift had most of the veteran Marine officers and NCOs (noncommissioned officers) in his division, the majority of the other men were high-spirited youths who had stormed the recruiting offices right after the attack on Pearl Harbor. Spirited though they might be, they didn't know too much about soldiering.

Nevertheless, General Vandegrift got ready for battle in one of the great shoestring operations in history. In fact, that was what his staff officers called the planned assault in the Solomons— Operation Shoestring. The Marines knew little more about Guadalcanal than what could be learned from a short story by Jack London and a faded picture taken by a missionary many years earlier. The necessary equipment had to be scraped together from all directions. The moment the transports arrived in Wellington, New Zealand, they were hurriedly unloaded and then

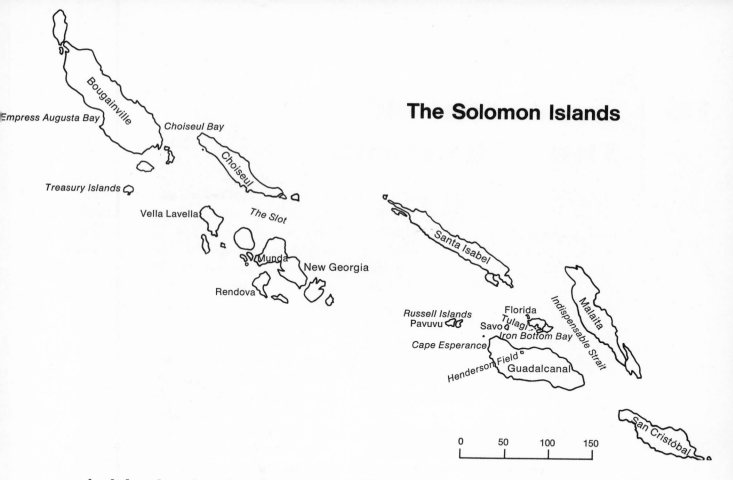

The Solomon Islands

reloaded with nothing but "beans and bullets," as war supplies are called. This was done during driving rains, for it was then winter "Down Under."

But Vandegrift got ready. He borrowed a regiment from another division and had 19,000 Marines aboard ship when the convoy stood out of hill-girdled Wellington Harbor on July 22.

August 7 the Marines attacked. Exactly eight months to the day after Pearl Harbor, the great American counter offensive was under way.

On the main island of Guadalcanal there was very little action. The force of laborers who were there fled into the jungle-covered mountains the moment American naval shells began crashing among them.

There was a fierce, bloody fight on

Tulagi and the twin islands of Guvutu-Tanambogo. Here the Japanese were dug in. Here, too, they launched the first of those wild "Banzai!" charges which never once overwhelmed the Marines. These were night attacks that got their name from the Japanese habit of screaming "Banzai!"—"Ten Thousand Years Forever!"—as they charged.

During the Marines' first night on Tulagi, the Japanese gathered in the darkness and struck with a howl. The Marines cut them down. They riddled the enemy with small-arms and machine-gun fire, while their mortars and artillery dropped shells among them. Sometimes the Japanese penetrated the Marine lines. Then there would be hand-to-hand struggles. As men rolled over and over in the blackness, they felt for each

81

U.S. Marines charge ashore on Guadalcanal Island.

other's throats or lashed out with knives. But the Marine line held. Next morning the Americans carried out the job of "mopping-up" Tulagi.

Guvutu-Tanambogo also fell, after the Marines blew the holed-up Nipponese out of caves by rushing to the cave mouths and hurling explosive-tipped poles inside them.

The battle was now to shift to Guadalcanal, where it would last for six months.

Though beautiful when seen from the sea, the island of Guadalcanal proved to be a mass of slops and stinks and pestilence. Her swamps were full of huge lizards, giant crocodiles, and stinging, sucking, slithering things. Her jungles teemed with snakes, centipedes, scorpions, crabs, and spiders. Clouds of flies rose from the rotting flesh of many of these creatures, as later they would rise from the heaps of slain soldiers. Mosquitos brought the fires of malaria and dozens of unknown diseases equally as agonizing or as deadly.

All over the island was the reeking odor of decay. The rain fell in torrents or the sun shone with near-equatorial intensity. In jungles that either dripped or steamed, the men of Nippon and of America were drenched or scorched by turns. And they were nearly always hungry, because the great air and sea battles taking place around them had the effect of denying them the supplies they needed.

Although the battle had begun favorably for the Americans, it soon swung sharply the other way. As soon as Vice Admiral Gunichi Mikawa heard of the American landings he led a Japanese surface force down The Slot. This was the watery corridor running between the Solomon Islands. Admiral Mikawa had five heavy cruisers, two light cruisers and one destroyer. He intended to slip up on the Americans and destroy their warships, after which he could sink their supply and troop ships at his leisure.

Mikawa's ships padded down The Slot in battle formation and stole silently past the American outpost ships. They crept up on round Savo Island rising from the harbor mouth like a brooding sentinel. It was not until nearly two o'clock in the dark morning of August 9 that an American destroyer began broadcasting the frantic alarm:

WARNING, WARNING, STRANGE SHIPS ENTERING HARBOR!

The warning came too late.

Three Japanese float planes dropped flares. The American warships were bathed in unearthly light. Japanese torpedoes which had been launched miles up The Slot struck the Australian cruiser *Canberra* with roaring crashes. Torn apart, *Canberra* had to be scuttled. The Japanese ships switched on their searchlights. They pinned hapless American ships in these great yellow beams and battered them into blazing wrecks. *Quincy*, *Astoria*, and *Vincennes* joined *Canberra* on the bottom. *Chicago* had her bow blown off. A destroyer was also sunk.

Historians call this engagement the Battle of Savo Island. Sailors and Marines who were there call it The Battle of the Five Sitting Ducks, which seems to be more descriptive of what happened. Savo was an inglorious disaster. The only comfort to be taken from it was that Admiral Mikawa did not tarry to sink the transports as he might easily have done. But in the morning the Marines looked out at Iron Bottom Bay —as the harbor was to be called because of all the ships sunk there—and saw that it was empty.

The Marines were all alone.

The struggle for Guadalcanal was now a defensive battle. The Japanese were determined to fight for the island. All General Vandegrift's men could do was hang on against overwhelming odds until reinforcements—land, sea, and air— could be rushed to the island.

Living off captured, wormy rice, the Marines were bombed all day long and then shelled at night from the sea. Often the shelling was preliminary for a night attack on land.

The first of these attacks came two days after the August 7 landings.

Lieutenant General Haruyoshi Hyakutake, who commanded Japanese soldiers in this area, had a very low opinion of Americans as fighters. He thought that approximately a thousand men would be enough to oust the Marines from Guadalcanal, and this was the number he sent down The Slot under Colonel Kiyono Ichiki. The Ichiki Detachment landed secretly at night on Guadalcanal, and Colonel Ichiki wrote in his diary: "18 Aug. The landing. 20 Aug. The March by night and the battle. 21 Aug. Enjoyment of the fruits of victory."

But they were bitter fruits. The Ichiki

83

Detachment tried to cross the Tenaru River by charging along a narrow sandspit. The Marines killed all but a handful of them. Next morning Colonel Ichiki burned his colors and shot himself in the head.

The next big land battle occurred three weeks later. About 4,000 Japanese soldiers came at night against a force of about 400 Marines under Colonel Merritt ("Red Mike") Edson. This was the most important of all the battles. If the Japanese took Bloody Ridge they would be able to overrun Henderson Field behind it. This airfield, of course, was the reason the Americans wanted desperately to hold Guadalcanal.

The Japanese did not succeed in their drive to Henderson Field, though they came alarmingly close to victory. At one point the Marines were forced to pull back to the crest of their ridge while Red Mike Edson called down a whistling, smashing barrage of artillery upon the onrushing Japanese. The barrage was so close that some of the shells fell among the Marines. A major named Kenneth Bailey rallied faltering men by grabbing them by the shoulder and yelling, "You—do *you* want to live forever?"

In the end the Marines held, and the Japanese attack was broken.

Still General Hyakutake up in the big enemy base at Rabaul, on the island of New Britain, continued to feed his units piecemeal into the overall struggle. If he had waited until he had collected all of them for one big thrust, he might have won. Late in October, 1942, he made his third big attempt at a position held by a battalion under Lieu-tenant Colonel Lewis B. ("Chesty") Puller. Once again the charging Japanese were slaughtered in the darkness. This fight lasted for two days, with Puller raging along the battlefront, roaring his commands. "We don't need radios," one Marine boasted. "We got Chesty!" Toward the end, a newly arrived battalion of soldiers helped throw back the Japanese.

This victory crowned a day of fire and destruction known as Dugout Sunday. Throughout the day there were so many Japanese airplanes dropping bombs or dog-fighting with Marine fliers, so many Japanese artillery shells falling within American lines, and such a heavy Japanese bombardment from the sea that very few men dared come above ground. But the Americans eventually won on all fronts.

The final victory owed much to a little band of courageous Marine fliers known as the Cactus Air Force. Like the gallant R.A.F. fliers in the Battle of Britain, these cocky young men in baseball caps and shoulder holsters made a contribution to the battle far beyond their numbers. They, too, fought for week after week without rest—but under far worse living conditions. They ate rice like their comrades in the foxholes, and they lived right in the center of the Japanese bull's-eye—much-bombed Henderson Field. But the Cactus Marines greeted each new day by rising to do battle in their stubby, powerful Wildcat fighters. These planes were not so fast as the Japanese Zeros and could not meet them in single combat. Flying in pairs, though, the Wildcats were invincible. Led by such

Major Joseph J. Foss

Major John L. Smith

sharp-shooting, high-flying pilots as Major John Smith and cigar-smoking Joe Foss, the Marines eventually wrested control of the air away from the Japanese.

Meanwhile, other events were contributing to a final crisis on Guadalcanal.

On October 18 Vice Admiral William ("Bull") Halsey relieved Admiral Ghormley as commander of the South Pacific Area. This meant that perhaps the most aggressive admiral in the United States Navy was in charge of the entire Guadalcanal operation. Bull Halsey was known throughout the Pacific as a man who loved to carry the fight to the enemy. He had already led carrier strikes against Wake, Marcus, the Gilbert and Marshall islands, and had commanded the ships that took Colonel Doolittle's raiders to Tokyo. So the battered Americans on Guadalcanal were heartened when they heard that Bill Halsey had taken over. A few days later Admiral Halsey told General Vandegrift, "I promise you everything I've got."

Halsey kept his promise.

On November 12 Vice Admiral Richmond Kelly Turner arrived with Army reinforcements. He quickly learned that a huge Japanese force was steaming down The Slot. The big battleships *Hiei* and *Kirishima,* the cruiser *Nagara,* and fourteen large Japanese destroyers were going to pour a ruinous bombardment on Henderson Field. This was to clear the way for the arrival of a big invasion force of soldiers. The Japanese were putting all they had into this last big effort.

To stop this formidable enemy fleet, Admiral Turner had only five cruisers and eight destroyers under the command of Rear Admiral Daniel Callaghan. They were badly outgunned. Nevertheless, Turner told Callaghan he must stop the Japanese—if only for one night. The damaged carrier *Enterprise* had been repaired and was racing north with a load of planes which would be able to attack the enemy invasion force. These planes would need to land on Henderson Field. Therefore, the field must not

85

Admiral William F. Halsey (left) with an aide aboard the USS Missouri.

Marine General Alexander Vandegrift (right) and Admiral Richmond Turner plan a raid on a Japanese base on Guadalcanal.

be wrecked.

Admiral Callaghan formed his force in battle array. At two o'clock in the morning of November 13 he stood on the bridge of his flagship, *San Francisco*, and shouted:

"Commence firing!"

Thus began the Naval Battle of Guadalcanal, one of the most fierce surface sea fights in all history.

The American ships headed straight toward the orange-flaming guns of the big Japanese battleships. "We want the big ones, boys," Callaghan cried. "We want the big ones!"

Little destroyer *Liffey* took on a big one. She ran in under great *Hiei's* mighty 14-inch turrets and peppered her bridge with 5-inch shells. *Hiei's* pagoda-like towers seemed to sway above her. Then *Hiei's* guns thundered, and *Liffey* began to burn.

Hiei thundered again.

A full salvo of 14-inch shells tore into the *San Francisco's* bridge. Gallant Daniel Callaghan fell dead. Another American admiral—Norman Scott—was killed aboard the cruiser *Atlanta*. But the Americans kept on charging and firing, plunging in and out of the smoke, pressing the attack—driving the invaders back.

Every ship but one of the United States fleet was hit. But so was every Japanese. The American cruisers *Juneau* and *Atlanta* were sunk, but so were two big enemy destroyers. Most momentous blow of all: the mighty *Hiei* was in her death throes.

Hiei sank later in the day, while fliers from Henderson Field and from the decks of the newly arrived *Enterprise* roared aloft to hunt out and pounce upon the helpless ships of the Japanese invasion force. This was a disastrous day for Japan. Nearly a whole division was destroyed at sea by the fliers of "The Buzzard Patrol."

On the night of November 14, Admiral Bull Halsey risked his new 16-inch battleships, *Washington* and *South Dakota,* to strike at a second Japanese bombardment force. Admiral Willis Augustus ("Ching") Lee brought the battleships into Iron Bottom Bay and into flaming collision with the Japanese battleship *Kirishima* and heavy cruisers *Atago* and *Takao. Kirishima* was sent to join *Hiei* on the bottom. *Atago* and *Takao* were put out of action for months.

Iron Bottom Bay was once again American. The exhausted Marines and the soldiers who had joined them a month earlier were now truly saved. Soon command on Guadalcanal passed from the Marine General Vandegrift to Major General Alexander Patch of the Army. General Patch mounted the offensive which drove the Japanese from Guadalcanal. On February 9, 1943, Japanese resistance ended.

To the north, a combined United States-Australian offensive had only recently defeated the Japanese forces at Buna-Gona in New Guinea. Originally Japan had hoped to seize Port Moresby in New Guinea and Guadalcanal in the Solomons. With these two bases—one in the north and the other in the south—the Japanese would have isolated Australia. But Japan had called off her waterborne invasion of Port Moresby after the Battle of the Coral Sea. Instead, Japanese troops entrenched on the opposite coast of New Guinea attempted to take Port Moresby by an overland drive across the towering Owen Stanley Mountains.

The Australians slowly drove them back. The Japanese then entrenched themselves in the Buna vicinity, and there the Aussies and the Yankee soldiers of the United States 32nd Infantry Division fell upon them in annihilating fury. By January 22, 1943, the entire Buna-Gona beachhead was in Allied hands.

General Douglas MacArthur's road back to the Philippines was now open. Just as important, the United States Navy had regained mastery of the waves, and control of the air was also passing to the Americans.

By February of 1943 the Rising Sun of Nippon had begun to set in the Pacific.

17 | The Road to Mandalay

Although Japan's sun had begun to set at sea, it was some time before Nippon could be driven from Burma and the threat to both China and India could be removed. In this area of combat—the China-Burma-India Theater—some of the least-known and least-glorified battles were fought. It was warfare at its worst—a savage, reeking, dripping style of fighting that raged for three years.

Most of this action took place in Burma, which the Japanese had wrested from the British in early 1942. Burma was important not only for its resource riches but also for its location. Burma lay between India, with her teeming millions, and Japanese-held Thailand. Holding Burma, the Japanese could invade India. They could also cut the famous "Burma Road" that linked India with China and the Chinese armies of General Chiang Kai-shek.

The Japanese did cut the Burma Road, thereby severing General Chiang's supply line to India. A force of British and Indian troops was defeated, as well as two Chinese armies commanded by a colorful American officer, Lieutenant General Joseph W. Stilwell. General Stilwell was nicknamed "Vinegar Joe" because of his sharp tongue. He did not hesitate to use it on himself. After the Japanese had forced him to make his

China-Burma-India Theater of War

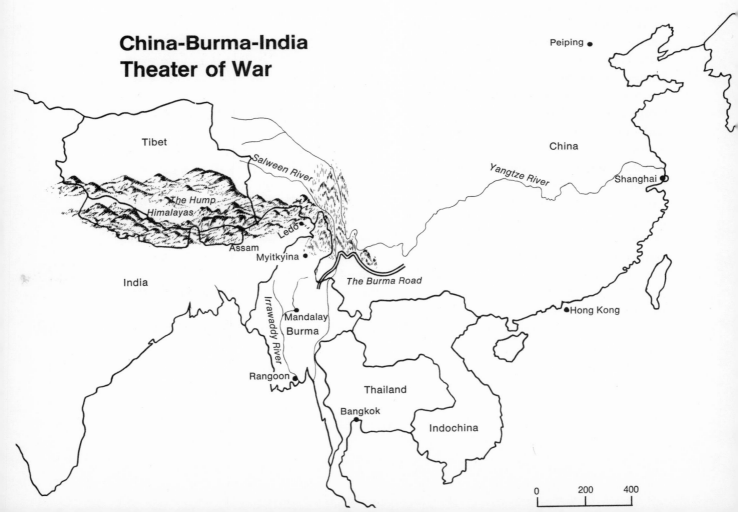

epic retreat from Burma into Assam across the Indian border, Vinegar Joe bluntly announced: "The Japs ran us out of Burma. We took a beating!" That was in May of 1942.

For the next two years the Allies were mainly concerned with getting supplies to General Chiang, who was still fighting the Japanese in China. Sending supplies by sea was out of the question, since the Chinese coast was in Japanese hands.

So American transport pilots began flying materials "over the Hump," the towering Himalayan Mountains separating northern India from China. Some of these peaks are as high as 24,000 feet, and the unarmed transports had to be wary of enemy fighter pilots. But they persevered. In the meantime, the famous "Flying Tigers" whittled away at the Japanese air power.

The Flying Tigers were daredevil American volunteers who had signed up to fight for China against Japan even before the United States entered the war. They had been recruited from the United States Army, Navy, and Marine air forces by a former American Air Corps captain, Claire L. Chennault, who had joined Chiang Kai-shek's staff. Schooled in the unconventional air-combat tactics of their unorthodox leader, the flamboyant and courageous Flying Tigers racked up some of the most impressive air-victory records of World War II. And many of their names —among them David Hill, Edward Rector, Robert Neale, James Howard, and George McMillan—became known throughout the world.

After America entered the war, the

Somewhere in the Burmese jungle General "Vinegar Joe" Stilwell and his guard take a ten-minute break.

Tigers either returned to their former branch of service or joined the United States Fourteenth Air Force. Chennault became a United States general, in command of the Fourteenth Air Force.

Meanwhile, General Stilwell was busy training Chinese troops flown into India, and at the same time conducting a savage guerrilla war against the Japanese in Burma. Most of this fighting against the Japanese was carried on by the "Chindits" of British Brigadier Orde Wingate and the American soldiers known as "Merrill's Marauders." The Chindits were named after the Burmese word for lion, *chinthé,* and the Marauders after their commander, Brigadier General Frank Merrill. All of them had volunteered for Burma.

The Chindits, supplied by air, struck at Japanese communications or destroyed bridges and supply dumps, but the Marauders had a more specific mission. While Stilwell's Chinese attacked the Japanese front lines, the Marauders slipped around the enemy's rear to set up roadblocks and cut off their retreat.

As the air-raid warning sounds, a group of Chennault's Flying Tigers streak toward their planes.

In the jungles of northern Burma, a survey party on elephants passes a bulldozer at work on the Ledo Road.

Such tactics kept the Japanese off balance in Burma, while the supplies flowing "over the Hump" and the onslaughts of American airmen slowed up the Japanese timetable for conquering China.

Meanwhile, in December of 1942, work began on a new supply road to China. This was the Ledo Road, an engineering marvel winding 478 miles over rugged mountain ranges from Ledo in India to Myitkyina in Burma. (Eventually this new road was to hook up with the old Burma Road into China.) American engineers supervised thousands upon thousands of Chinese laborers working with hand tools and baskets.

As the Ledo Road literally inched south toward Myitkyina, it became necessary for the Allies to wrest that area from Japanese hands. The Myitkyina attack was led by General Stilwell, under the overall command of the British Admiral Lord Louis Mountbatten, the new chief of Southeast Asia Allied Forces. Although Stilwell's drive opened in early 1944, Myitkyina did not fall to the Allies until August of that year. The Japanese had launched an offensive of their own, and the Allies driving down toward Myitkyina collided with the Japanese thrusting up toward India. In the end, it was Allied air superiority which made the difference.

After the fall of Myitkyina, the Japanese were driven steadily back toward Thailand. On January 7 of 1945 the Ledo Road was completed and within another month the Japanese had been hurled out of Burma for good, removing the threat to India.

North Africa: | 18
Hitler's First Defeat

Before the attack on Pearl Harbor, the military chiefs of America and Britain had agreed that Germany would be the number one enemy, even if Japan entered the war. Once Hitler and his partner, Mussolini, were defeated, all the Allied power would be brought to bear on Japan. Even Russia, which had not declared war on Japan, might do so then.

The terrible disaster at Pearl Harbor interfered with this plan. The Americans decided that Japan must be halted, or at least held at arm's length, before they could make good on their promise to defeat Hitler first. Eventually Admiral King managed to bolster Pacific striking power to the extent that the Japanese suffered a decisive defeat at Midway and then were driven from Guadalcanal. With this accomplished, the bulk of American military power shifted back to the primary enemy, Germany.

In Europe the Soviet army was still fighting desperately against the German invaders. During August of 1942 the German Sixth Army had begun the siege of Stalingrad, the epic battle of the Eastern Front. To help embattled Russia, the United States had already begun sending supplies by sea over three routes.

The most dangerous route was the so-called "Murmansk Run," along the coast of Norway and around into the Arctic Ocean and the ports of Murmansk

and Archangel. There were terrible losses on this route. Out of one convoy of thirty-two ships only ten made port at Murmansk. Not only U-boats but long-range Nazi bombers based in Norway struck at these convoys.

Less dangerous was the "Persian Corridor," which took convoys around South Africa and the Cape of Good Hope and up the Persian Gulf to ports in Iran. The supplies were then unloaded and shipped overland to Russia.

Safest of all was the route through Japanese-controlled waters to Vladivostok in Siberia. These supplies were usually carried by ships flying the Soviet flag. The Japanese still had a neutrality treaty with Russia and they let these ships alone.

But if Russia knew her proper battlefield, the British and Americans could not agree on theirs. The British wanted to hit the Germans on the outer ring of their new empire. They wanted to bleed Germany white until enough men and forces could be gathered for a knockout blow. To do this they would keep jabbing at the outer ring while starving Germany with the naval blockade and wearing her down with air bombing. The British had already, in May of 1942, begun massive night raids on German cities. The first of these was the thousand-bomber attack on Cologne.

In opposition to this the Americans proposed a single massive stroke hurled

91

across the English Channel through France and into the heart of Germany. Premier Stalin of Russia supported this proposal. He even sent Foreign Minister Molotov to Britain and the United States to urge the opening of a "Second Front" in France immediately. Stalin was not embarrassed by the fact that he had not objected to the German victory in France in the days when he was Hitler's friend. All he cared about now was to have a front reopened there so that Hitler would have to move troops from Russia to France.

To satisfy the Russians, a British-Candian force staged a reconnaissance in force at Dieppe on the French coast in August of 1942—the same month the Americans were invading Guadalcanal. The German drove the attackers off, killing or wounding more than half of them.

Near-disaster at Dieppe helped to convince the British military chiefs that there were not enough men and arms available to invade France in 1942. Britain had already been thrown out of Europe three times: from France, Norway, and Greece. If she came back a fourth time, she wanted to be sure of staying. In 1942 the British army was still small compared to its navy, and the United States Army was far from full strength. Moreover, it would be another six months before United States industrial production would overtake the Axis output.

President Roosevelt agreed with Mr. Churchill that the Allies were not ready for an invasion of the Continent. But he was most eager that Hitler should be attacked somewhere soon. North Africa was finally agreed upon as the target.

But then came the calamitous succession of Japanese victories in the Far East. In addition, the U-boat war broke out anew, and Britain's Eastern Mediterranean Fleet was reduced to three cruisers and a few destroyers. The North African invasion had to be postponed. It was not scheduled again until the Desert War had gone through another of its dramatic about-faces.

Actually, the Desert War in North Africa was such a seesaw kind of battle that the people who lived there were said to keep two sets of flags handy. They would pull down the Swastika and raise the Union Jack at the approach of the British, only to hoist up the Swastika again with the return of the Nazis.

Mussolini's men had been the first to invade British-held Egypt, but they had been stopped at Sidi Barrani. Then General Wavell threw them back out of Egypt in the famous Desert Gallop. Next, Rommel arrived and drove the British back into Egypt, after which a British general named Auchinleck pushed Rommel back and reëntered Libya, coming to the relief of beleaguered Tobruk.

In the spring of 1942, on a moonlit night, Rommel attacked again. His armor sprang forward and raced toward Tobruk. The garrison hung on doggedly, but these men were not the immortal "Rats of Tobruk" who had held out for eight months. On June 21 Tobruk fell to Rommel. The hard-driving Afrika Korps pressed on, driving toward Cairo and the Suez Canal.

Winston Churchill was in Washington at the time. He told Mr. Roosevelt of Tobruk and the impending disaster in the desert.

"What can I do to help?" the President asked.

"Send us as many Sherman tanks as you can spare, and ship them to the Middle East as soon as possible."

The President sent for General Marshall and told him of Mr. Churchill's request.

"Mr. President," said the General, "the Shermans are only just coming into production. The first few hundred have been issued to our own armored divisions to replace old equipment. It is a terrible thing to take the weapons out of a soldier's hands. Nevertheless, if the British need is so great, then they must have them. And we could let them have a hundred 105-millimeter self-propelled guns besides."

Placed aboard ship almost immediately, three hundred American tanks and one hundred guns were rushed to Egypt even as Rommel's armor clanked forward toward final victory. Then a new

General Sir Bernard L. Montgomery

British tank crews in Africa clamber onto their Sherman tanks.

commander was placed in charge of the British Eighth Army, the force of British, Anzacs, Poles, Indians, Czechs, and Free French which had supplanted the old Army of the Nile. General Bernard L. Montgomery was a wiry, waspish man who wore a tank-trooper's beret. He was fond of talking in sporting terms, and he could inspire great devotion in his men. They called him "Monty."

The moment General Montgomery took over, he told his men there would be no retreat from their position at El Alamein in northern Egypt. "We will fight on the ground we now hold," he said, "and if we cannot stay here alive, we will stay here dead."

Monty's men held at El Alamein. Triumphant, General Montgomery began building his forces for his own breakout.

Now a North African invasion became more urgently needed than ever before. The Anglo-American forces could land at the rear of the Axis army even as Montgomery's Eighth Army was battering at its front. If the enemy forces were destroyed, the threat of an Axis hookup with Japan would be removed. The Brit-

93

Behind a dense smoke screen, Australians prepare to rush a German strong point during the fighting at El Alamein.

ish lifeline into the Far East would be safe, and ships now making the long slow voyage around the Cape of Good Hope would save forty-five days by sailing directly through the Mediterranean. Moreover, control of North Africa would give the Allies a base from which to invade Italy.

So an Allied invasion of North Africa was finally scheduled for November, 1942. And an American officer, Dwight D. Eisenhower, was named Commanding General, European Theater of Operations. Eisenhower had already achieved an excellent reputation for his staff work in the Philippines (before the war) and in Washington. Soon he would command the African invasion forces.

In the meantime, General Montgomery at El Alamein was still building up his forces. Monty was in the situation he loved best, getting ready for the "prepared" battle. The opposing army was now commanded by General Georg von Stumme, because Rommel had become ill and gone home for a rest. Monty studied his rival's weaknesses, putting his infantry, armor, and air power into

position like a man tidying a chess board. On October 23, 1942, he told his troops:

"When I assumed command of the Eighth Army I said that the mandate was to destroy Rommel and his army, and that it would be done as soon as we were ready. We are ready *now!*"

In bright moonlight that night, the Battle of El Alamein—the final thrust of the Desert War—was launched with a roar.

A thousand big guns, massed hub-to-hub, began thundering at the German positions. The night sky trembled and shivered to ten thousand flashings. Even mortars and machine guns joined the terrible onslaught on the Germans' advanced infantry positions. The barrage went on for four hours. After it had lifted, the foot soldiers sprang to their feet and charged forward. Their high battle cries sounded strangely thin in comparison to the full-throated roaring that had just ceased. Then came the probing of light armor. By morning there were two corridors cleared through the enemy mine fields.

Montgomery hurled his heavy assault formations into the battle.

The action became widespread and confused. General von Stumme, Rommel's replacement, rushed to the battlefield. He fell dead of a heart attack, and the tide of battle began flowing strongly against the Germans.

Adolf Hitler heard the ominous news in his northern headquarters. Called the "Wolf's Lair," it was located at Rastenberg in Prussia. Immediately the Fuehrer telephoned General Rommel at his sanatorium. Would the Desert Fox return to the Desert? Though still ailing, Rommel said he would go. He left immediately by airplane, arriving the night of October 25.

But one general, however skillful, could not change the outcome. The Eighth Army had gained that complete mastery—especially in the air—which becomes irresistible in the hands of a commander such as Montgomery. Rommel personally led one counterattack which failed and weakened his forces for Montgomery's renewed blows.

The German general ordered a full retreat.

The British pursued. Streaming backward along the Libyan coast, the Germans and their Italian allies were bombarded from the sea by the British navy and savaged from the skies by the Royal Air Force.

The Battle of El Alamein was an Allied victory. As Winston Churchill later said: "Before Alamein we had never had a victory, after Alamein we never had a defeat."

Then there came even greater news: the Americans were invading North Africa!

There were actually three invasions of North Africa on that momentous morning of November 8, 1942.

One was at Casablanca in Morocco on the Atlantic coast; the others were inside the Mediterranean Sea—at Oran and Algiers in Algeria. The invasion force sailed to the battle from bases in Britain and the United States. It in-

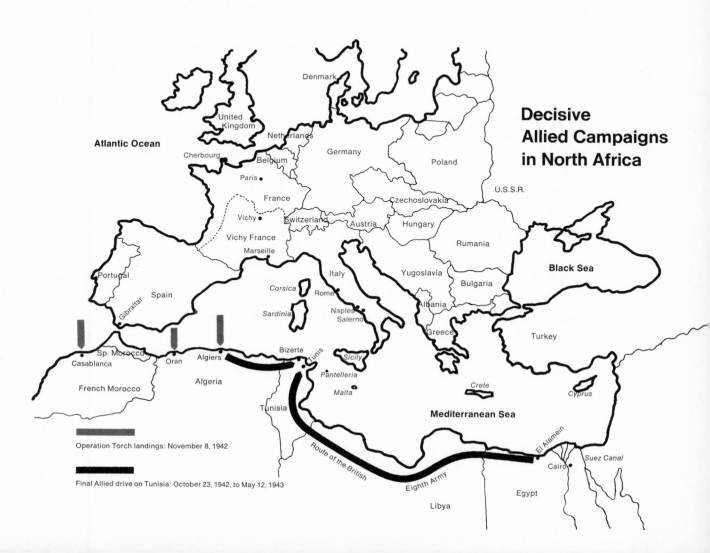

Decisive Allied Campaigns in North Africa

Operation Torch landings: November 8, 1942

Final Allied drive on Tunisia: October 23, 1942, to May 12, 1943

cluded 105,000 men, of whom 23,000 were British and 83,000 were American. The Americans formed almost all of the assault waves, for there was hostility to Britain in the French-held lands of Morocco, Algeria, and Tunisia. Many French officers resented British attacks on the French fleet after the fall of France. At that time, the British had also given naval support to an attack delivered against Dakar in French North West Africa by General Charles de Gaulle and his Free French. This had caused the Vichy Government to bomb British bases in Gibraltar and to regard Britain as an enemy.

How the French army would react to Allied landings in North Africa was General Eisenhower's greatest worry. He hoped that the French would join the Allies or at least not fight them. To achieve this hope, he planned to appeal to traditional French-American friendship. This was why only Americans would be in the spearhead.

General Eisenhower made two other attempts to win the support of the French army. He sent Major General Mark Clark on a secret mission to Algeria. Tall and hawk-nosed, Clark was the officer whom Winston Churchill called "the American eagle." In Algeria he was to meet two French generals known to be sympathetic to the Allies. Accompanied by a few aides, Clark sailed by submarine to the Algerian coast. The craft surfaced at night. General Clark and his band inflated rubber boats and paddled ashore. Dripping wet, they slipped off into the darkness. They had brought with them a sum of

money to be used to organize sympathy for the Allies.

The Americans met Generals Mast and Bethouart at the rendezvous area, but suddenly the French police swooped down on the meeting and broke it up. In making their escape the Americans lost their money. But finally General Clark and his band succeeded in reaching their waiting submarine. All he had to report for his efforts was that a widespread sympathy for the Allies seemed to exist among lesser French generals and admirals.

For General Charles de Gaulle there was only dislike and suspicion. De Gaulle had repudiated Marshal Pétain's surrender, had escaped to England and set up the Free French Government. Many French officers in North Africa felt that, if General de Daulle was right, then they were wrong. This they could not accept. Instead, they chose to regard de Gaulle as disloyal to his soldier's oath.

Casting about for a leader whom the French might follow, the Allies thought of General Henri Giraud. He was virtually a German prisoner in southern France. But they managed to communicate with him. He slipped out of his jailers' hands and made his way to the coast. There, on a dark night, he stepped into a small boat and headed for a waiting submarine, which took him to a flying boat. General Giraud was then flown to Eisenhower's headquarters in Gibraltar.

The moment this tall, stiff, stern soldier met General Eisenhower and heard of the invasion plan he assumed that he had been rescued to command it. Ike was thunderstruck. He tried to explain that he wanted General Giraud to come to North Africa with him in order to bring French forces over to the Allied side. Giraud shook his head. "Giraud will be a spectator in this affair," he insisted, causing the Allied commanders to go to bed with long faces.

Next morning, however, the French general changed his mind. He agreed to accompany the expedition in the capacity Eisenhower had offered him.

That night General Eisenhower and his staff stood on the dark Gibraltar headlands peering down anxiously on the first of hundreds of Allied invasion ships steaming through the narrow Strait of Gibraltar. It was a critical moment. At any instant the ships might begin to flame and explode under enemy submarine attack. But there was none.

Early the next morning—November 8, 1942—the invasions began.

At Algiers, the farthest penetration within the Mediterranean, almost immediate success greeted the American soldiers and Rangers who came storming ashore. The capital city of Algeria surrendered on the first day.

About 130 miles west at Oran there was fierce resistance. Moreover, General Eisenhower discovered to his dismay that the French leaders in North Africa had no intention of taking orders from General Giraud. Many of them still considered Vichy their rightful government. A long bloody battle seemed in the offing. Then came unexpected news.

Admiral Darlan was in Algiers visiting his sick son.

General Dwight Eisenhower (left) with French General Henri Giraud.

If there was one man the French would obey it was Jean Françoise Darlan. He had already been designated as Marshal Pétain's successor in Vichy. Disliked though he was by both the British and American governments, he was the one man who could end the bloodshed. General Clark conferred with him in Algiers.

At first Admiral Darlan refused to order his countrymen to lay down their arms. But then on November 10 he issued an order for the French to cease resistance. When Pétain objected, Darlan rescinded the order. But after he heard that Hitler had used the North African landings as an excuse to invade southern France, he changed his mind again. The occupation of southern France violated Hitler's treaty with the Vichy Government. Finally, on November 13, Eisenhower flew to Algiers and a final settlement was arranged. Admiral Darlan would be political head of all North Africa, and all hostilities were to cease.

The fiercest fighting of all had been raging at Casablanca. The invasion force there was commanded by Major General George S. Patton, or "Old Blood and Guts," as he was affectionately nicknamed by his men. Tall and deep-chested, General Patton was truly a soldier to behold. His general's stars gleamed on his helmet; his polished boots sparkled, and his famous pearl-handled revolver dangled from his hip.

Patton's invasion force had been under fire even before their feet touched Casablanca's sand dunes, for the French battleship *Jean Bart* was hurling 15-inch shells at the invading fleet. Her guns were finally silenced by American dive bombers, but the French army units ashore kept on fighting. Eventually it was necessary to throw tanks into the fray.

Then the invasion force decided to bomb Casablanca itself. Navy Dauntlesses roared aloft from the carrier *Ranger*. They came winging over the city, circling, circling, circling, awaiting the word to pounce.

Fortunately Darlan's November 10th order arrived just in time to stop the fighting. The French navy surrendered, and the bombing attack was called off. The authorities in Casablanca accepted Darlan's order as official.

On November 11, 1942, three days after the invasions began, Casablanca capitulated. The French commanders met General Patton, who read the sur-

American troops debark from transports and enter the assault boats that will take them to the shores of North Africa.

render terms to them. They objected. They were convinced that the treaty, by destroying the French Military Protectorate in Morocco, would introduce chaos in the country. General Patton paused to think. Then he tore the treaty to pieces.

"Gentlemen," he said, "I had the pleasure of serving with your armed forces throughout two years of World War One. Needless to say, I have implicit faith in the word of honor of a French officer. If each of you in this room gives me his word of honor that there will be no further firing on American troops and ships, you may retain your arms and carry on as before—but under my

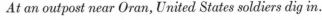

At an outpost near Oran, United States soldiers dig in.

98

orders. You will do thus and so. We will do this and that. Agreed?"

The Frenchmen nodded.

Although the North African invasion was now considered a stunning success, there was no time to waste. Once the problem of French allegiance had been solved, General Eisenhower sent his forces racing to Tunisia.

Tunisia was the land separating Algeria from Libya. In Libya, of course, General Rommel's army was retreating with General Montgomery's forces in hot pursuit. Eventually Rommel would reach Tunisia, where he would be joined by the reinforcements which Hitler was already rushing to North Africa. If Rommel received sufficient reinforcements, he might turn and fall upon Montgomery.

General Eisenhower's purpose was to get an Allied army to Tunis ahead of Rommel.

But the weather and the rapid build-up of German forces in North Africa saved Rommel for the winter. When General Eisenhower visited the Tunisian front on December 24 he was appalled by sights which he has described himself:

"The rain fell constantly. We went out personally to inspect the countryside over which the troops would have to advance . . . I observed an incident which . . . convinced me of the hopelessness of an attack. About thirty feet off the road, in a field that appeared to be covered with winter wheat, a motorcycle had become stuck in the mud. Four soldiers were struggling to extricate it but in spite of their most strenuous efforts succeeded only in getting themselves mired into the sticky clay. They finally had to give up the attempt and left the motorcycle more deeply bogged down than when they started.

"We went back to headquarters and I directed that the attack be indefinitely postponed. . . ."

Given such a breathing space, it was not long before General Rommel went over to the counterattack. He struck at an American force in the vicinity of the Kasserine Pass and drove them back. But the assault lost momentum, and the Germans were themselves forced to retreat.

Now the North African campaign became a race between General Montgomery's Eighth Army closing in from the south and General Eisenhower's in the north. Rommel realized that the battle was lost, but Hitler would not let him evacuate his forces.

The end came on May 7, 1943, when the British First Army under General Sir Kenneth Anderson smashed into Tunis and the American II Corps under General Patton crashed into Bizerte. Rommel himself had been recalled earlier by Hitler for other duties, but a quarter-million German and Italian soldiers and their officers were herded off to prison compounds.

North Africa had fallen. The Suez Canal was safe. The Mediterranean was now an Allied sea, and Italy herself lay open to invasion. Only three months after the American triumph at Guadalcanal, a decisive victory had at last been won by Allied arms in the struggle against Mussolini and Hitler.

19 | Death of the Wolfpacks

In mid-January of 1942—a month after the Japanese attack on Pearl Harbor—the German U-boats had opened a furious assault on American coastal shipping. Operation "Roll of the Drums," the Germans called it, and throughout that dreadful year the sound of torpedoes striking home off the eastern coast of America did sound like a funeral tattoo for United States sea power.

Enemy submarines lay on the bottom by day and went hunting by night. They fired their torpedoes from the sea toward ships silhouetted against the bright lights of coastal cities. The American east coast was a shameful blaze of light from Atlantic City to Miami. The resort cities said a coastal blackout would "ruin the tourist season."

So ships were sunk and sailors drowned by the light of boardwalks and ballrooms. Not until May was a dim-out ordered on the sea front.

Meanwhile, the U-boats grew bolder. They even attacked in daylight on the surface; they were so confident and elated at their success. They called the first six months of 1942 "the happy times."

Admiral Doenitz boasted: "Our submarines are operating close inshore along the coasts of the United States of America. . . . bathers and sometimes entire cities are witnesses to . . . the red glorioles of blazing tankers." This was tragically true. On June 15 thousands of bathers at Virginia Beach watched in horror while a German U-boat torpedoed two American freighters. Eastern beaches were crusted with oil scum and littered with the debris of sunken ships that had been washed ashore. American seamen passed through a terrible trial of suffering and death, especially men aboard torpedoed tankers. They could not swim through the thick scum of oil on the sea's surface. If it became ignited by a signal flare, then they were engulfed in a sea of fire.

In the first half of 1942, five hundred and sixty-eight Allied ships were lost at a cost of only fourteen enemy submarines. General Marshall notified Admiral King: "The losses by submarines off our Atlantic seaboard and in the Caribbean now threaten our entire war effort."

There were other dangers, among them the giant German battleship *Tirpitz*. This warship—the largest in the world at the time—could give trouble merely by being in existence. One large Arctic convoy to Russia was scattered and massacred just because of reports that the *Tirpitz* was steaming to the attack. Other German surface ships, such as the battleship *Scharnhorst*, offered a similar challenge. Before the end of the year, though, *Scharnhorst* was sunk in a pitched sea battle against British warships. And British bombers eventually put *Tirpitz* on the bottom.

As always, however, the U-boat war

Fire rages on an American tanker torpedoed off the East Coast.

was the greater peril. Admiral Doenitz was obtaining many big new submarines. Huge tanker or supply submarines, which the Allies called "milch cows," were developed to keep the combat boats in food and fuel. And eventually a snorkel or breathing device was introduced. It enabled U-boats to stay submerged as long as they liked.

Admiral Doenitz himself was always equal to each new Allied challenge. When anti-submarine measures became successful in one area, Doenitz shifted his attack to another. In July, 1942, he sent the wolfpacks into the Caribbean. Then they appeared in the South Atlan-tic off the bulge of Brazil. Toward the end of the year they were prowling the North Atlantic again.

Doenitz had discovered that Allied air power could not patrol the entire Atlantic. There was a point at mid-ocean where convoys had no air cover. The wolfpacks massed there. November, 1942, was the blackest month. Allied sea power had been drawn off to the landings in North Africa. The U-boats sank 117 ships in November!

During the entire black year of 1942 the Allies suffered the loss of eight million tons of shipping. U-boats were sinking ships faster than the United States could build them.

America was faced with two tremendous challenges. First she had to replace Allied shipping losses, and then double the replacement if enough munitions were to reach the fighting fronts. Next she had to build warships especially designed for protecting this new fleet of merchant ships.

New shipyards were opened all over the country, and a novel, easily built type of cargo vessel was designed. This was the Liberty ship, which President Roosevelt laughingly called "an ugly duckling." The Liberties were ugly, and they were slow and uncomfortable. But they could be built quickly. This was their chief virtue. Their parts were prefabricated—made in different factories and then brought to the shipyards to be put together. Gradually American industrial know-how cut construction time from thirty-five weeks for the first

Twin geysers shoot skyward as a U.S. Navy PT boat drops two depth charges. These speedy little patrol craft fought valiantly to drive German U-boats from American shores.

Liberty ship delivered in 1941 to an average of five weeks per ship in late 1942. In all, 2,700 Liberty ships were constructed, and they carried 75 per cent of America's cargo across the seas during World War II.

Protecting them were new fleets of sleek destroyer-escorts and a new little aircraft carrier known as the CVE. The CVEs carried sixteen fighter planes and twelve torpedo bombers. Screened by the sub-killing destroyer-escorts, the CVEs became the scourge of the wolfpacks. All the newly developed detection devices were put at their disposal. Sighting a submarine, the fighters attacked by dropping depth charges, and the Avengers launched torpedoes. Toward the end of the war the "Fido," or homing torpedo, was developed. Dropped anywhere near a U-boat it would unerringly head for the submarine's steel hull.

The escort carriers filled the gap in Atlantic air cover that had worked to Admiral Doenitz's advantage.

Gradually, as the Allies became more expert in hunting and killing submarines, the undersea war turned against the Germans. By mid-1943 German shipyards were struggling to replace the losses in Admiral Doenitz's fleet. The Admiral himself waged the war relentlessly, but he could not replace the most serious losses of all: seasoned U-boat skippers. His own two sons and his son-in-law went to the bottom, along with others such as Gunther Prien, who had struck one of the first blows of the war by sinking a British battleship in Scapa Flow.

In February of 1943, just as the Rising Sun of Japan began setting in the Pacific, Adolf Hitler's lucky star plummeted into the snow and ice of the Russian city of Stalingrad.

At this great industrial center on the banks of the Volga River the Fuehrer made his final bid for victory in Russia. If he could possess Stalingrad—named after Premier Josef Stalin himself—he would deal a great blow to Russian morale. He would also capture valuable factories and seize oil supplies needed for Moscow and Leningrad in the north.

On August 22, 1942—only a day after the Americans on Guadalcanal won their first pitched land battle over the Japanese—Adolf Hitler announced:

"We are attacking Stalingrad, and we shall take it."

There were about 300,000 German soldiers—the flower of the Wehrmacht— under General Friedrich von Paulus. They attacked after a pulverizing air and artillery bombardment had flattened three-quarters of the city. But the very success of their bombardment slowed down their advance. German tanks could not move through rubble-choked streets. Gradually, in growing numbers, Russian soldiers and civilians armed with knives and guns and grenades came flowing out of smashed and splintered buildings in vicious counterattacks.

The epic battle of the Eastern Front was under way.

It was a titanic struggle which raged for months. Thousands died daily. To bury them was impossible. The dead of both sides were gathered up and burned en masse. From his new headquarters in the Russian Ukraine, Hitler was on the verge of hysteria as he urged his generals on. From Moscow, Stalin issued daily bulletins, all ending: "Death to the German invader!"

When it became clear to General von Paulus that his Sixth Army could not capture Stalingrad that year, he tried to persuade Hitler to allow him to withdraw. The Fuehrer was enraged. "Stand and fight!" he ordered. "I am not leaving the Volga."

In November, 1942, Hitler announced that Stalingrad had fallen. "Only a few small sectors are not yet in our hands," he said. A few days later a Soviet army under General Georgi Zhukov came out of these so-called few small sectors in an overwhelming counterattack. Two far-ranging Russian spearheads got behind the Germans. They joined, and General von Paulus and his Sixth Army were trapped.

Then winter set in.

The German soldiers began to freeze and starve. They were forced to eat frozen horses, dogs, and cats. From jubilant Moscow came this broadcast, ominous to German ears:

"Every seven seconds a German soldier dies in Russia. Stalingrad is a mass grave."

There were dreadful casualties among the Russians, too, but the Soviet Union realized that it possessed superior numbers. Premier Stalin was willing to trade a Russian life for a German life, for he knew he had an almost inexhaustible supply. As one German officer said: "The German army in fighting Russia is like an elephant attacking a host of ants. The elephant will kill thousands, perhaps even millions, but in the end their numbers will overcome him, and he will be eaten to the bone."

While the white beast of winter howled about them, the German soldiers began to send home pitiful letters:

"My hands are done for, and have been ever since the beginning of December. The little finger of my left hand is missing and—what's even worse—the three middle fingers of my right one are frozen. I can only hold my mug with my thumb and little finger. I'm pretty helpless. . . ."

"Of the division there are only sixty-nine men still fit for action. Bleyer is still alive, and Hartliebe as well. Little Degen has lost both arms. . . ."

"We have no winter clothes. . . . We have been swindled and have been condemned to death; we shall die of the war or of frost."

To hear of such complaints, or to hear his generals again request permission to fall back and re-form, was enough to goad Hitler into fury. By January, 1943, however, it was no longer possible to withdraw. The original Sixth Army force of about 300,000 men had been whittled

Russian soldiers with automatic rifles drive Nazi soldiers out of houses in the outskirts of Stalingrad.

German troops photographed after their surrender at Stalingrad.

down to about 80,000 caught in an ever-narrowing circle of steel, fire, and ice. On January 8 the Soviets demanded that von Paulus surrender. He relayed the ultimatum to Hitler and received this reply on January 24:

"Surrender is forbidden. Sixth Army will hold their positions to the last man and the last round."

There were not many men or rounds left, and on January 31 Sixth Army headquarters got off its final message:

"The Russians stand at the door of our bunker. We are destroying our equipment. This station will no longer transmit."

On that day von Paulus surrendered to the Russians the miserable remnant of his once-proud German army.

The turning point had now arrived on the Eastern Front. Germany by herself had been dealt a defeat which was the disastrous equal of the one dealt to Germany and Italy together in North Africa. It was a calamity brought on by Hitler's fanatic pride. He believed himself invincible, and had been willing to sacrifice hundreds of thousands of men to prove it.

After Stalingrad, the Soviet army fell upon the Germans with a roar of tanks and artillery. The remainder of 1943 witnessed a parade of Russian victories. Before the year was out, most of the lost territory had been recovered; and the Russians were within striking distance of Poland. By then Adolf Hitler was back in his Wolf's Lair, turning his gaze south to behold Allied arms once more on the continent of Europe.

21 | The Allies Invade Italy

In early January of 1943—while the Anglo-American armies hammered the Axis in North Africa and the Russians destroyed the Germans at Stalingrad—a momentous meeting was held at Casablanca by President Roosevelt, Prime Minister Churchill, and the combined staffs.

At this Casablanca Conference the United Nations, as the Allies were now called, outlined the final plan for crushing the Axis. It was decided that Italy would be invaded after North Africa fell. This move would not only get at the Axis from the south but would also relieve some of the German pressure on Russia. Also, all possible supplies were to continue to be sent to Russia. Meanwhile, the Anglo-American mass bombing of German industry was to be stepped up, and forces were to be gathered in England for the cross-Channel invasion of France the following year, 1944. Finally, the Japanese would be contained in the Far East.

Prime Minister Churchill later carried this plan to Premier Stalin and received his approval. Stalin also approved the "Unconditional Surrender" of the Axis demanded by President Roosevelt, who said:

"The elimination of German, Japanese, and Italian war power means the unconditional surrender by Germany, Italy, and Japan."

This proposal was to prove trouble-some, because Hitler used it to convince his people they must fight on to keep the Allies from enslaving them. It was criticized in England and America for just that reason. But it was never withdrawn. Unconditional Surrender became the final Allied objective. Germany, Italy, and Japan were to be made to give up. There would be no terms or bargaining. The Axis armies would have to lay down their arms and throw themselves upon the mercy of their conquerors.

Four months after this proclamation, the Axis force in North Africa had been destroyed. It was now possible, during the summer of 1943, to carry out the proposed invasion of Italy.

The first step was the seizure of the big island of Sicily lying in the Mediterranean between the tip of Tunisia and the toe of Italy. On Sicily were 405,000 Axis troops—315,000 Italians and 90,000 Germans. Against them General Eisenhower planned to send only 180,000 Americans and Britons, with their allies from Canada, Poland, France, and Brazil. Usually an invasion force likes to have a 3-to-1 edge in numbers, but this Allied army had other superiorities: in tanks and artillery and vehicles, in the sea and air power. Moreover, General Eisenhower was a believer in "hitting them where they ain't." He knew that the best Axis formations—the German ones, which included the first-rate Hermann Goering Division—were massed in the west of Sicily. So the Allies were going to land in the south and east.

But first, the island fortress of Pantellaria had to be knocked out.

Pantellaria, lying between Tunisia and Sicily, had an airfield from which the invasion could be menaced. It was also a tiny and impregnable rock held by 11,000 Italian soldiers whose guns were "zeroed-in" on the one small harbor through which landings might be attempted. Nevertheless, General Eisenhower wanted Pantellaria. He thought he could get it cheaply, for he believed that most of the Italian troops had had enough fighting "and were looking for any good excuse to quit."

The General was right. A fierce Allied air bombardment, lasting six days and nights, battered Pantellaria to its knees. More scared than injured, the Italian garrison climbed out of their bomb shelters and surrendered to the invading forces without a fight. That was on June 11, 1943.

The following month was spent in bombing Sicily. Meanwhile, a huge invasion armada was steaming in from far-off bases in the United States and England. It massed at close-up points along the Mediterranean. Airborne troops also assembled. To bring so many troops and ships and planes from so many different places was a difficult and complicated operation. But it was done. Veteran campaigners from North Africa were also withdrawn for this new operation.

On the morning of July 10, the soldiers of the Allied nations went sloshing

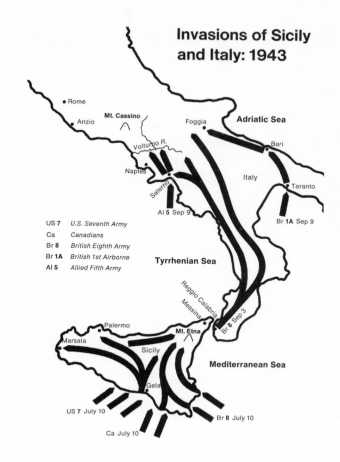

Invasions of Sicily and Italy: 1943

US 7   *U.S. Seventh Army*
Ca   *Canadians*
Br 8   *British Eighth Army*
Br 1A   *British 1st Airborne*
Al 5   *Allied Fifth Army*

through tumbling white surf to storm the ancient shores of Sicily. General Montgomery's Eighth Army and the Canadians landed on the right, General Patton's United States Seventh Army came ashore on the left.

They were all but unopposed.

As calculated, the Axis commander, Field Marshal Albert von Kesselring, had massed his forces far to the west. And Allied paratroopers who had landed during the night had held up the Hermann Goering Division as it raced to the landing area under orders to throw the invaders into the sea. This feat of arms was accomplished despite heavy

General George Patton (pointing) lands at Gela, Sicily, with men and officers of the U.S. Seventh Army.

losses among the British airborne force. Many of the gliders were cut adrift too soon, and high winds blew the men into the ocean.

Otherwise, the landings were a success. General Montgomery began punching north toward the chief city of Messina. Part of General Patton's men began a westward dash around the coast while another column drove straight north across the center of the island. The opposition began to stiffen. The Germans showed themselves masters at the art of digging antitank traps. On one side of the road they would dig a deep hole about twenty feet long and ten feet wide. Then they would cover it with chicken wire and dirt to make it look like the road. About fifty feet beyond on the other side of the road they would dig another trap. Then they would put barbed-wire barricades in front of each trap so as to tempt the tank commander into butting it down and crashing through the chicken wire into the pit.

Such tactics slowed the Allied ad-

vances. But General Patton's free wheeling troops clattered on. Eleven days after the landing they cut the island in half and rattled into Palermo. General Patton has described this event:

"As we approached, the hills on each side were burning. We then started down a long road cut out of the side of a cliff which went through an almost continuous village. The street was full of people shouting, 'Down with Mussolini!' and 'Long live America.'"

So it went as the Americans pursued the hated Germans. Flowers were strewn in the liberators' path, and gifts of wine, lemons, or melons were pressed upon them. Italian soldiers began surrendering in thousands. Soon the Americans had joined forces with General Montgomery on the right. A continuous Allied line surged steadily forward against the German defenders fighting from the mountainous northeast corner of the island.

The Germans fought stubbornly. Retreating slowly, they blew up bridges and destroyed narrow shelf roads snaking around Sicily's steep cliffs. The pursuing Allies had to press mule trains into service. Engineers clung to the sheer cliff faces like human spiders as they built trestles that would support the advancing Allied spearheads.

Then the Germans began evacuating troops across the Strait of Messina into Italy. The Allied pursuit became a race for Messina, which General Patton's men won. On August 17, 1943, the entire island fell to the Allies. And on that same day there were American 155-millimeter rifles or "Long Toms," as the GIs

Infantrymen advance along a Sicilian cliff near Capo Calava.

called them, hurling shells across the Strait against the mainland of Italy.

Even before the landings in Sicily, the Italian mainland had been brought under massive aerial bombardment. The crash of those bombs undermined the government of Benito Mussolini.

By then the Italian dictator was a hated man. Most Italians blamed him for the bombing of their country, for the widespread hunger and misery induced by the war, for the loss of an empire in North Africa, and for the death of hundreds of thousands of young Italians. All of these calamities were recited in propaganda leaflets which Allied aircraft dropped over Rome and other big Italian cities on July 17, 1943. The final

Searching for enemy snipers, an Allied reconnaissance unit makes its way through the smoke from burning buildings in Messina.

paragraph of that leaflet said:

"The time has now come for you, the Italian people, to consult your own self-respect and your own interests and your own desire for a restoration of national dignity, security and peace. The time has come for you to decide whether Italians shall die for Mussolini and Hitler—or live for Italy, and for civilization."

Signed, ROOSEVELT
CHURCHILL

The message struck home. It gave encouragement to a group of Italian leaders led by Marshal Pietro Badoglio. They plotted Mussolini's downfall.

Fearful of this, Mussolini flew off to a meeting with Adolf Hitler just two days later. He pleaded for help. The Fuehrer replied with a pep talk and an explanation that Germany needed all it possessed for the Russian front. Even

as they talked Rome was bombed.

Mussolini rushed back to his capital. Five days later he was forced to call a meeting of the Fascist Grand Council. It was the first such gathering since 1939. Frantically Mussolini tried to bully the Council into giving him a vote of confidence. But the. Council voted instead that he must turn over command of the armed forces to King Victor Emmanuel III.

Next day, July 25, Mussolini hurried to see the King at the Villa Savoia. Angry, the dictator shouted that the Grand Council had no right to censure him. The King disagreed.

"Then," Mussolini thundered, "according to your Majesty I ought to *resign*."

"Yes," the King said calmly, "and I accept your resignation forthwith."

Mussolini was stunned. He had hoped to bluff his way through. He seemed on the verge of collapsing.

"Then my ruin is complete," he muttered hoarsely, and tottered from the King's presence.

Outside, Mussolini found himself under arrest. He was forced aboard a police ambulance and taken, eventually, into imprisonment on the island of Ponza. In his place, the King appointed Marshal Badoglio.

General Mark Clark and a fellow officer on an inspection tour of front line positions in Italy.

Now the way was clear to talking peace with the Allies. All of Italy had been overjoyed at the fall of the hated Mussolini. Italians wanted to get out of the war. But Marshal Badoglio wavered. He was afraid the Germans would take over the country if they suspected what he was up to. He also feared that the Allies, having already proclaimed Unconditional Surrender, would lay down harsh terms which would send the emotional Italian mobs foaming off in another direction.

Badoglio arranged secret meetings with Allied agents in Spain, Portugal, and Sicily. He made all kinds of counter proposals to Unconditional Surrender. He asked that a huge invasion force land in Italy the day he surrendered. He demanded full details of such an invasion. But General Eisenhower could not agree, and when the Allied commander ordered the bombing attacks to be resumed Badoglio surrendered his country.

This was done on September 3, 1943, the day that the Allies began landing in Italy.

The first landing was made by two divisions of General Montgomery's Eighth Army. They crossed the narrow strait between Messina and Reggio di Calabria on the toe of the Italian boot and began a fighting march up the east coast. Their objective was Foggia and the Luftwaffe air bases there.

On September 9, 1943, the United States Fifth Army under General Mark Clark assaulted the beaches of Salerno on the west coast. General Clark's mission was to strike north to seize the big city of Naples with its enormous harbor.

111

If the landing was successful, an Allied column would be driving up each of the coasts of Italy.

The day after the Salerno landings, however, Allied fortunes began sinking. All hope for an easy conquest of Italy faded when the Germans occupied Rome and began fortifying the northern hills. Worse, by then Field Marshal von Kesselring had convinced Hitler that Italy could be held against the Allies. He said he could throw a series of defensive lines right across the peninsula. He would fight and fall back from line to line and make the Allies buy every yard with blood. Hitler approved this proposal. Then he had Mussolini plucked from the hands of his captors in a daring rescue.

The former dictator had been moved from the island of Ponza to a hotel in the mainland hills. In mid-September a force of elite German soldiers crash-landed a glider near the hotel and overwhelmed Mussolini's guards. Brought to northern Italy in safety, he proclaimed a puppet government which took orders from the Fuehrer.

At Salerno, meanwhile, disaster impended. General Clark had hoped for surprise. But as the GIs in assault boats roared shoreward through the early-morning darkness, a loud-speaker began crackling ashore and a German voice said in English:

"Come on in and give up. You're covered."

They *were* covered. German artillery was emplaced on all the high ground looking down on the beachhead from the left, front, and right. A terrible kill-

ing barrage was poured onto these crowded, pebbly beaches. But the GIs fought bravely inland. They crawled through barbed wire and wormed their way around machine-gun nests to toss grenades at them from the rear. They knocked out tanks with bazookas. They brought their own tanks and self-propelled guns ashore and gradually seized the appointed ground.

Four days later the Germans counterattacked, driving the Fifth Army back. General Clark rushed to the front and told his soldiers: "We don't give another inch. This is it. Don't yield anything. We're here to stay."

Though the Fifth Army stayed, their situation was perilous for a few days, especially after von Kesselring hurled his tanks into the battle. They burst through the American lines and began carving out pockets in the rear. But von Kesselring did not mass his six hundred tanks for a single blow. That was his big mistake. Aided by Allied bombers flying in from North African and Sicilian bases, the soldiers at Salerno held out.

After Montgomery's slow but steady drive up the east coast threatened to turn the German left flank, von Kesselring fell back on Naples. Then the Eighth Army captured Foggia. Now Allied aircraft had bases right on the edge of the battle. On October 1 the Fifth Army entered Naples. They found a blackened, ruined city. The Germans had tried to destroy one of the oldest cities of civilization.

Reservoirs were drained, telephone exchanges dynamited, and tunnels through the hills were blown up. Bus and railway systems had been wrecked, and time bombs and booby traps were strewn throughout the city to slaughter civilians as well as soldiers. Hotels had been burned down, while prisons were thrown open, flour mills demolished, and hospitals looted. The ancient University of Naples had been deliberately set on fire, and bishops and abbots carried away as hostages. The harbor was clogged with sunken ships, and its docks were ruined, smoking skeletons.

Even so, Allied engineering skill was equal to the enormous task of bringing order out of chaos. Within a month the harbor was partially cleared and supplies were being unloaded. Civil affairs officers were soon busy caring for a hungry and horror-stricken population. These officers were especially trained for such a mission, and had been used effectively for the first time in Sicily.

Meanwhile, the double-barreled Allied advance up the coasts of Italy was bogging down. Marshal von Kesselring had given Hitler wise advice when he urged a defensive battle in northern Italy. The terrain was made for such warfare. It was a jumble of steep hills, chasms, gorges and narrow, winding valleys. Cold, swift rivers fed by Alpine lakes raced through the valleys, twisting and turning back on themselves so frequently that one United States division crossed the Volturno River several times in a single advance. "Every durn river in this crazy country is named Volturno," a GI jeep driver complained.

And winter in "sunny Italy" could be very, very bitter. Rains fell in torrents, washing out bridges or undermining roads, turning the hillsides into slops of cold, coarse mud. On the high ground above every gorge or valley were well-emplaced Germans, who poured a steady withering fire into creeping lines of British and American troops. Only the rain forests or heat-bathed coral islands of the Pacific could rival the Italian front for sheer misery.

The only way to dislodge the enemy was by direct assault. There was no room for maneuver. Tank tactics were of no use. Great masses of men could not be sent suddenly sweeping around the enemy to cut him off or encircle him. It was blow for blow, shot for shot, while bearded, grimy, mud-caked men crept up hills or went rolling down them, locked in mortal struggle with the enemy.

Thus the Italian campaign became enmired in a toe-to-toe slugging match. And then there came a change of command. General Eisenhower was called to England to plan the great cross-Channel assault scheduled for spring of 1944. The British General Sir Harold Alexander took Ike's place. There was no change in the battle, however. Marshal von Kesselring was making good on his promise to Hitler.

But as the Italian campaign ground slowly down in mud and misery, the long-stalled counteroffensive in the Pacific blazed up anew.

22 | Japan Retreats

The war against Japan was vastly different from the war against Germany and Italy. The Pacific War was an "island war." Japan had planned to keep her stolen empire safe behind a long line of island forts. For the Allies to burst in upon this empire, to get to Japan herself, it was necessary to break through the island barrier.

Early in the war the two American commanders in the Pacific—General MacArthur and Admiral Nimitz—both decided that it would be foolish and costly to attempt to capture every one of hundreds of fortified islands. Instead they chose to take the most important ones and by-pass the others. The Japanese garrisons of the by-passed islands were to be left to "wither on the vine." If they possessed airfields which might menace the American rear, these would be rendered useless by constant hammering from American air and sea power.

General Tojo later admitted that this "island-hopping" strategy was one of the chief causes of Japan's defeat. The Japanese had acquired these islands one at a time, and they thought that the Americans would want to do the same.

The island-hopping advance to Japan was to follow two routes. One led westward straight across the Central Pacific through the thousands and thousands of tiny islands before veering right or north toward Japan. This route was fol-

lowed by the forces under Admiral Nimitz. The second or Southwest Pacific route ran through what is called the Bismarcks Barrier. This barrier is formed by the island of New Guinea on the left and the Solomon Islands and the island of New Britain on the right. Beyond the Bismarcks Barrier lie island stepping stones to the Philippines. This second route was the one followed by General MacArthur, beginning with Guadalcanal in the Solomons and Buna-Gona in New Guinea.

Then came a lull in the Pacific land fighting. All the soldiers and equipment—especially the vital landing boats—were being shipped to North Africa, Sicily, and Italy. There were some small actions, though.

A few weeks after Guadalcanal fell, Marines landed unopposed in the Russell Islands farther up the Solomons chain. In May, far to the north, American soldiers retook the Aleutian Islands off the coast of Alaska. The Yanks fought in deep snow drifts to destroy the Japanese on Attu Island, and when a force of Canadians and Americans landed on Kiska they were surprised to find that the Japanese had fled. By mid-August the Aleutians were in American hands.

These actions, of course, were relatively small. But the war that raged in the skies above the Southwest Pacific was very large indeed. It never let up. Fortunately for the Americans and their

Australian and New Zealand allies, there were new types of aircraft in the Pacific by this time. The Army Air Forces had the long-range, twin-tailed Lightning fighter and the Liberator bomber, which could carry more bombs for a longer distance than the Flying Fortress. The Navy and Marine fliers had the Hellcat fighters, a big improvement over the old Wildcats, and the Marines also prized the new Corsair. This was a paddle-bladed, gull-winged fighter plane that could do anything better than the Japanese Zero. And of course there were the improved versions of the old Dauntless dive bombers and Avenger torpedo bombers.

American fliers were also better trained. This was proved on March 1, 1943. That day a Japanese convoy was sighted in the Bismarck Sea off New Britain. Six transports and two freighters escorted by eight destroyers were bringing reinforcements to Japanese strongpoints on New Guinea. Word was quickly flashed to the Allied Air Forces in Port Moresby.

Flying a shuttle over the towering Owen Stanley Mountains, approximately a hundred Allied planes poured destruction on the convoy. Here is a bomber pilot's typical report of that fierce onslaught:

"When within strafing range I opened fire with my forward guns. The decks were covered with troops, lined up facing the attacking plane with rifles in hand. However, my .50-calibers outranged their small arms and I saw hundreds fall and others go over the side. . . . I then ceased fire and I made a gradual pull-up to clear the masts. My bombs skipped into the side of the ship and exploded, leaving large hole at the waterline."

In this action, which became known as the Battle of the Bismarck Sea, all of the Japanese troop and supply ships and half of the destroyers were sent to the bottom. Never again did Japan risk big ships in supplying either New Guinea or cut-off garrisons in the Solomons. Barges were used instead. They moved at night, hiding out in coves by day. Eventually the barge traffic would also be destroyed under the combined blows of aircraft and torpedo boats. American fliers struck at the holed-up barges by day, while the PT boats hunted them by night.

Meanwhile, Admiral Yamamoto plotted revenge. He collected 350 airplanes, at that time an enormous number. Their mission was to blast American bases and sink American shipping and so cripple the Yanks that Japan would have time to strengthen the Bismarcks Barrier. The first thunderbolt was hurled at Guadalcanal.

On the afternoon of April 7, 1943, sixty-seven Val dive bombers and one hundred and ten Zeros came roaring down The Slot. Only seventy-six American fliers rose to meet them, but they made a mockery of Yamamoto's "revenge." They shot down twenty-one Japanese planes and badly damaged many others with a loss of only one American pilot. Seven of the enemy planes were knocked from the skies by Lieutenant James Swett, a 22-year-old Marine flier out on his first combat

A formation of Lockheed P-38 "Lightnings."

flight. His feat remained one of the most remarkable performances of the war.

After the Guadalcanal fiasco, Yamamoto shifted to New Guinea for his revenge. The Japanese pilots did no better there, but they returned reporting great success. To "save face" the Japanese fliers would often pretend to have done better than they actually had. Their commanders would then be led into a false feeling of security. This was what happened to Admiral Yamamoto. Satisfied, he called off his great revenge operation. Then he scheduled a trip to the big island of Bougainville in the Upper Solomons.

American intelligence learned of the trip.

Because they had broken Japan's secret code, the Americans knew the exact time Yamamoto was scheduled to arrive. A "killer" band of twelve Lightning fighter planes was assembled. The morning of April 18 they flew up The Slot. Their timing was perfect. They arrived just as Admiral Yamamoto's transport began to lower for a landing. The Lightnings tore into Yamamoto's cover of nine Zero fighters while the "trigger section"—the best shots—flashed down for the kill. Captain Thomas Lamphier caught Yamamoto's transport in his sights. His wing guns stuttered, sawing off the enemy plane's wings. The transport plunged into the jungle, killing Yamamoto.

Yamamoto's intended revenge for the Battle of the Bismarck Sea had turned into an American revenge for the attack on Pearl Harbor.

The blows against the Bismarcks Barrier began to fall with sledgehammer force. General MacArthur struck from the left, moving along the New Guinea coast; and Admiral Halsey, under MacArthur's orders, swung from the right along the Solomons ladder.

General MacArthur's first three objectives were the Japanese strongholds of Salamaua, Lae, and Finschhafen on the Huon Peninsula. He already had a force of Australians marching east over mountains toward Salamaua. To help them, he decided to strike from the south with an American force. The last day of June a group of versatile torpedo boats led a force of Yanks toward Salamaua. The soldiers were in open landing craft and they set sail in the teeth of a howling wind and over heavy seas. But they landed at a point approximately sixteen miles below Salamaua. From there they began battering the Japanese with artillery, and then joined the assault. From east and west two forces were now converging on Salamaua.

Next MacArthur struck at Lae. Although these operations were never large compared to most of the European invasions, they were by any standard models of precision and daring. At Lae MacArthur again planned two assaults. The waterborne one was composed of Australian soldiers and American sailors. The morning of September 4, 1943, American destroyers battered palm-fringed beaches about fifteen miles east of Lae. Then the Aussies paddled ashore in rubber boats, to be followed by larger numbers in landing craft. The Australians wheeled west and began marching on Lae.

The next day American paratroopers jumped onto a Japanese airstrip to the west of the village. General MacArthur watched this operation from a transport. The Yank paratroops seized the strip, and Australian and American engineers soon made it big enough to receive larger craft. Twenty-four hours later, transports flew in thousands of Australian "diggers," as the Americans called those dashing, slouch-hatted soldiers. This force now began marching east.

From west and east, two forces converged on Lae. The Japanese commander realized that defeat was inevitable and fled into the jungle with his men. Many of them died of hunger or malaria. Lae fell to MacArthur on September 16.

Throughout these operations, the fliers of Major General George C. Kenney's Fifth Air Force blasted the Japanese air force from the skies and gave vital support to the ground troops. Bombardment ships of the United States Navy poured steel and fire upon the enemy, giving the Japanese their first taste of what their own navy had done to the Marines on Guadalcanal. Thus the American "triphibious" whip—the triple onslaught of air, sea, and ground power—was being brought to perfection.

At the next stop, Finschhafen, the Fifth Air Force simply pulverized the big enemy airbase at Wewak. The way was now clear for the United States Seventh Fleet to put Australians ashore. In the pre-dawn darkness of September 16, the Diggers drove a small Japanese force back from the beaches and seized a beachhead. The Japanese commander

117

had mistakenly believed that the assault would be overland. He had stationed most of his forces below and behind the town. MacArthur, the past master of "hitting them where they ain't," had scored again. By the time the Japanese recovered, they were unable to budge the Australians from their beachhead. By October 2 Finschhafen was safely in Allied hands. And the Japanese made no attempt to recapture it, because all of their strength was now directed toward holding off Admiral Halsey's advance on the right.

Fleet Admiral Mineichi Koga had succeeded the slain Yamamoto. He renewed the aerial war against Guadalcanal and the newly occupied Russell Islands. He massed hundreds of airplanes in the huge Japanese bastion at Rabaul on the eastern tip of New Britain. These he planned to send over the Russells to entice American fighters into combat. In this way, Admiral Koga thought, he would whittle down American air strength.

But the Yanks needed no enticement. They came boiling into the skies at the first alarms, and it was Koga's air force that was whittled down. In one great battle over the Russells—"the big hairy dogfight," as the Americans called it— 81 Zeros fought 110 Allied aircraft. Twenty-four Japanese were shot down against seven Americans lost. Such scores were typical.

A U.S. Army Air Forces plane, flying only a hundred feet above ground near Lae, passes over a disabled Japanese bomber. Under the tree, at right, lies an enemy Zero that will never fly again.

Even so, the Japanese still possessed a great advantage. The Americans had only two air bases—Guadalcanal and the Russells—but the Japanese had a string of them from the enormous complex at Rabaul down through the Solomons to the island of New Georgia. Admiral Halsey decided to take New Georgia.

His plan was set in motion by one of those romantic incidents characteristic of the Pacific fighting—a rescue call from an Australian coastwatcher named Donald G. Kennedy.

The coastwatchers had been among the most valued men in the Allied command. They were planters and sea captains who had gone into the hills when the Japanese invaded New Guinea and the Solomons. From their lookouts they kept watch of Japanese movements and radioed this information to Allied forces. Many a Japanese air strike on Guadalcanal failed because the coastwatchers had given the alarm and American fighter planes were "stacked" in the clouds waiting to pounce on the enemy. Coastwatchers also rescued American fliers who had been downed in the sea or the jungle, or sailors whose ships had been sunk. Lieutenant John F. Kennedy, later to become president of the United States, was helped by a coastwatcher, after the torpedo boat he commanded had been rammed and cut in two by a Japanese destroyer.

Of all the coastwatchers, Donald Kennedy on New Georgia was the most famous. He shot up the enemy's barges and ambushed their patrols. After they sent a large force against him, he faded into the hills and called for help.

Thus, on the dark night of June 20, 1943, two American destroyers picked their way through the dangerous waters off Segi Point at the southern tip of New Georgia. Ashore, Mr. Kennedy lighted bonfires to guide them, cheerfully signaling: "Okay here." At daybreak two companies of Marines went ashore. Their mission was to rescue Kennedy, and also to seize Segi Point as a base for an American airstrip.

That was how the invasion of the Central Solomons began.

On June 30 the United States Navy put a much larger force of American soldiers ashore on the island of Rendova. This mountain of land stood west of Munda Airfield on the island of New Georgia. After the Americans destroyed the enemy garrison of about three hundred men on Rendova, they put artillery into place. By seven o'clock that night they were firing on the Japanese across the channel on Munda.

A few days later the Americans slipped across the channel to land near Munda itself. Gradually these forces were built up until there was an entire Army corps—about 30,000 men—battling the Japanese around Munda Airfield. Although there were other landings and other expeditions on New Georgia, this was the most important one. And the most bitter. The Japanese were resolved to fight to the last man. They had built a wicked system of pillboxes. Two hard, grueling months passed before Munda fell to the combined onslaught of Marine tanks and Army infantry.

The island north of New Georgia in the Solomon chain is Kolombangara.

But Admiral Halsey leapfrogged this and took the next one, Vela Lavella. In the meantime, naval and air battles were raging all over The Slot and in the narrow straits and channels between the islands. The United States Navy was busy intercepting and sinking Japanese barges, as well as enemy warships. The Americans were also mining enemy waters. American fliers bombed the enemy bases, struck at Japanese fighter strength, or provided air cover for the landings.

By November of 1943 Admiral Halsey was ready for the biggest and northernmost of the Solomon Islands: Bougainville. General Alexander Vandegrift was in command of this invasion. He, too, believed in hitting them "where they ain't." He decided that the Japanese expected him to come at Kahili Airfield on the southern tip of the island. Instead, he chose to land at Cape Torokina, halfway up Bougainville's 130-mile coastline. There were only three hundred men there.

To deceive the enemy further, a New Zealand force landed in the Treasuries below and left of Kahili. Then a battalion of Marines landed at Choiseul, below and to the right of Kahili. They were under orders to "make a lot of noise." Meanwhile, Admiral Halsey announced that "a large force" had landed on Choiseul.

On the last night of October some 20,000 Marines sailed straight for Kahili, but then, under cover of darkness, they veered to the west and swung around the island to land at dawn on Cape Torokina.

The Japanese were taken by surprise and it was a long time before they mustered a force of about 40,000 men to counterattack the American beachhead. Their initial efforts all failed during some of the bitterest fighting, and amid some of the foulest weather, of the Pacific War. A United States Army division soon joined the Marines, and then another arrived.

In March of 1944 the Japanese were finally able to march their men through Bougainville's black jungle to make a mass assault upon Torokina. But it failed utterly.

Before that happened, Navy Seabees and Army engineers had been busy working miracles in the Torokina swamp. They built Torokina Airfield within three hundred miles of Rabaul.

From this famous strip American pilots roared aloft to join the terrible aerial bombardments which General Kenney's fliers were raining upon Rabaul from their bases in New Guinea. Among these doughty warriors of the air was the colorful Major Gregory ("Pappy") Boyington. Boyington's nickname was a result of his being a few years older than the young pilots he led in his Black Sheep Squadron. He had fought with the Flying Tigers in China. Like Major Richard Bong and Major Thomas McGuire of the Army Air Forces, he was a superb pilot and an excellent shot.

The flamboyant Pappy developed the fighter sweep. He led massed flights over Rabaul and taunted the enemy to come up and fight. Whenever they did, they were shot down in numbers far out of

Marines strive to maintain their beachhead on Bougainville.

proportion to American losses. Rabaul's air strength gradually weakened.

United States Navy air and sea units also struck repeatedly at Rabaul. After the Bougainville invasion, an American force defeated Japanese ships in the Battle of Empress Augusta Bay. The same week the carriers *Princeton* and *Saratoga* raced north to fly off planes which thundered suddenly over Rabaul's harbor and struck a crippling blow at Japanese sea power. Six days later, on November 11, a group of five fast carriers repeated the performance.

Rabaul was becoming a ghost base.

Yet this mighty bastion, standing at the right-hand end of the Bismarcks Barrier, was still too powerful to take by direct assault. It was heavily fortified at the water's edge and guarded by towering mountains from its rear. More than 100,000 Japanese soldiers defended Rabaul, and they would turn any direct assault into a terrible blood bath.

Again the Americans went leapfrogging. They struck at the western tip of the long island of New Britain, 370 miles away from Rabaul. First a regiment of dismounted cavalrymen were put ashore at Arawe on the southwest coast. They

Weary Marines on their way to a rest camp after twenty-three grueling days on the front lines at Cape Gloucester.

met only a handful of defenders.

Then, on the day after Christmas, 1943, a division of Marines assaulted Cape Gloucester on the same island, to seize its valuable airfield. Here the Marines attacked the Japanese in a series of violent battles, some of them fought at the height of howling hurricanes and in the full downpour of the monsoon. They killed five thousand of the enemy and captured five hundred, at a cost of fourteen hundred American casualties. The western third of New Britain was all in American hands by April of 1944. An iron ring had been drawn around Rabaul, and Allied air power was given the job of keeping this by-passed base permanently disabled.

It was General MacArthur, however, who delivered the blow that burst the Bismarcks Barrier for good.

To the north of Cape Gloucester lie the Admiralty Islands. MacArthur knew there was an airfield and a good harbor in the Admiralties, and the islands were well placed to support his stepping-stone push to the Philippines. The General decided to "inspect" them himself. A force of 1,000 cavalrymen was assembled to make this "reconnaissance in force." If MacArthur found the islands lightly defended, he would seize them.

But the Admiralties were not so lightly defended. Approximately two thousand Japanese fiercely resisted the outnumbered Americans. In charge after charge, they sought to drive them into the sea. MacArthur quickly ordered another regiment—the famous "Seventh Cav," General Custer's old outfit—into the battle. With the aid of destroyers hurling shells at the enemy in support of the final attacks, the Americans finally destroyed the Japanese force.

MacArthur's victory in the Admiralties came on March 9, 1944. By that time other American forces under Admiral Nimitz had burst through the outer ring of Japan's Central Pacific barrier.

Some of the most rugged battles in United States military history were fought during the advance through the Central Pacific, for Japan had turned her island chains into a series of ocean forts. Among them were some of the most heavily fortified fixed positions ever encountered by an invading force.

The chains of the Central Pacific were formed not by ordinary islands but by atolls. An atoll is a ring of coral islets enclosing a lagoon. The Japanese did not need to fortify all the islets of an atoll. They would choose the biggest one to hold an airfield from which airplanes might strike at American shipping or invasion forces. Then they would turn the islet into a bristling fortress to protect this airfield.

Both the seaward and lagoon waters would be filled with barbed-wire barricades, mines, and cement antiboat obstacles. Sometimes a sea wall approximately four or five feet high would girdle the islet. A man raising his helmet above this barricade would make as naked a target as a fly on a windowpane. Vast numbers of machine guns, rifles, and light artillery were interlocked to sweep the edge of the sea wall, and firing ports were cut in the wall for anti-boat guns. Mortars and other artillery were also zeroed in on all the boat approaches and beaches.

Farther inland there would be a network of pillboxes mounting antitank guns, interlaced with rifle and all kinds of machine-gun pits. Tanks would be buried hull-down in the sand or coral, creating makeshift pillboxes able to swivel cannon and machine guns in all directions. Many of these positions were connected by trenches or underground burrows. Finally, there would also be huge bombproofs with reinforced concrete walls five and six feet thick. Inside these were the fighting headquarters and sometimes coastal guns big enough to duel battleships.

Maneuver was just not possible in the Central Pacific. The only recourse was a straight-ahead charge. True enough, Army, Navy, and Marine pilots poured great masses of bombs on these island forts, and the Navy bombarded them weeks before and immediately prior to a landing. But bombs are only effective when they score direct hits, and most of the positions on these ocean forts were cleverly camouflaged. An American rifleman sitting on a hummock of sand wouldn't know he was actually on top of a pillbox until a gun slid out and began firing. So all depended on the bravery and fighting skill of the individual troops. Fortunately, when the Central Pacific advance was launched, these

Admiral Ernest J. King (front seat), General Holland Smith (standing) and Admiral Chester Nimitz make a jeep tour of a captured Pacific island.

qualities were found to exist in glorious abundance.

The first of the assaults was against the Gilbert Islands, lying about 2,400 miles west of Pearl Harbor. Admiral Nimitz chose Marine Major General Holland M. ("Howlin' Mad") Smith to command the attack. Using both Army and Marine troops, Smith assaulted the atolls of Makin and Tarawa on November 20, 1943.

Makin was quickly taken. Two United States Army regiments destroyed a force of three hundred soldiers and five hundred laborers in just a few days. A quick victory had been expected, however, because the Japanese had massed their defenses on Tarawa, where Betio

Islet, a tiny coral saucer of 291 acres, had been heavily fortified. Betio's commander, Rear Admiral Keiji Shibasaki, was so confident of his defenses that he boasted: "A million men cannot take Tarawa in a hundred years."

Approximately 12,000 Marines, drawn from Major General Julian C. Smith's 2nd Marine Division, assaulted Tarawa. Waves of assault troops in landing boats and amphibious tractors sailed from their transports into the lagoon. The first wave was transferred to amtracs—"little boats with wheels," the Japanese called them. Then the amtracs or amphibious tractors fanned out and bumped over the lagoon reef. They settled into the boiling water and roared toward Betio's sea wall.

The terrible thundering of the bombardment battleships outside the atoll lifted. American dive bombers flew home. Little Betio was obscured in dust. A glowing pink cloud hovered above her. The Marines were jubilant. An American admiral had promised their officers: "It is not our intention to wreck the island. We do not intend to destroy it. Gentlemen, we will obliterate it." His promise seemed fulfilled.

And then the Japanese gunners recovered from their initial shock and began shooting.

Bang! Whannggg! Baloom!

Amtracs blew up. Amtracs slewed and sank. Amtracs reached the beach only to burst into flames.

Marines in the water were riddled by machine-gun fire. They staggered ashore, some carrying wounded buddies. They reached the sea wall and huddled

A tank stalls as it tries to climb the sea wall during the invasion of Tarawa.

under it, only to be struck by enemy guns poking out of the fire ports. The amtracs returned to the reef to pick up the second assault waves waiting in landing boats. They were sunk as they went.

There were not enough amtracs to carry the men ashore, and the landing boats could not get over the reef. The Navy had made a dreadful mistake in calculating that there would be a high tide over the reef. There was not. The waiting Marines could see the coral.

They had to wade in.

They advanced straight into the withering enemy fire, their wounds dyeing the water red. Many fell into the water and drowned, overcome by wounds or the weight of heavy equipment. Still the Marines advanced into that hail of bullets. They emerged from the lagoon with their camouflage dungarees clinging to their limbs, and joined their embattled comrades under the sea wall.

More and more assault waves ran the gantlet of death. Soon the Marines were leaping the sea wall and attacking inland with rifles, grenades, and flame throwers. They jumped into the enemy pits and fought the Japanese gunners to the death. Then tanks joined the attack. They were ferried in by lighters or led ashore by brave guides, who felt through the water for potholes.

Colonel David Shoup, who commanded one of the regiments, struggled ashore. He had been wounded, but he

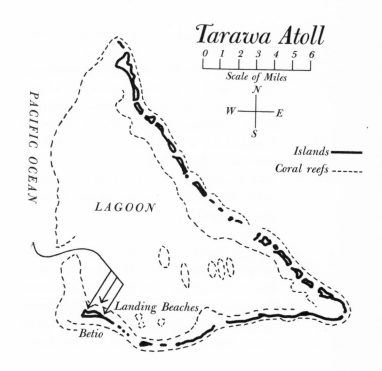

set up a Command Post right under the gun of an enemy pillbox. From there he directed the desperate battle.

Betio was now an inferno of heat and noise, over which billowing clouds of bombardment dust were drifting. Smoke and flames were everywhere. Reinforcements waded ashore, leaped the sea wall, and plunged into clouds of dust and smoke. The dust got in their eyes, ears, nose, and mouth, mixing with perspiration and becoming caked. The smoke choked the men. Still they fought on, gradually increasing their hold.

By nightfall the invaders had established only a handhold on the left and a toehold on the right. That night, all along the narrow beach under the sea wall, fearless Navy medical corpsmen tended to the wounded. Doctors carried out operations in captured pillboxes guarded by Marine riflemen. Sometimes the Japanese jumped into these makeshift operation rooms and were shot dead beside the operating table.

Throughout the dreadful night, the Americans braced for an enemy counterattack. But the Banzai charge did not come. Admiral Shibasaki could not communicate with his holed-up troops. Still confident of his defenses, he sat in his enormous bombproof headquarters. He was sure that, with the dawn, his gunners would make another day's slaughter.

They nearly succeeded, as they began raking a fresh wave of reinforcements. But by then the Americans ashore were driving to each side to knock out the enemy antiboat guns and beach positions. Soon the Marines, with their tanks, were driving across the island. By midafternoon, Colonel Shoup reported: "We are winning."

Next day the Marine advance was irresistible. Covered by riflemen, bulldozers rolled up to the exits of the pillboxes and heaped sand over them. They sealed off the gunports. Thus the Americans knocked out position after position. Coming to Shibasaki's bombproof, they fought a wild pitched battle on its roof. Eventually they seized possession of it, pouring gasoline down the air vents and dropping in hand grenades.

On the fourth day Betio fell. The bastion that was supposed to hold out for a hundred years against a million men had been taken in four days by 12,000 United States Marines—but at a dreadful cost. Soon the Seabees, the Navy's remarkable construction men, were at work on the atoll, building airfields for use in forthcoming Pacific invasions.

The next assault in the Central Pacific was against Kwajalein Atoll in the middle of the Marshalls, about 650 miles west of Tarawa.

Kwajalein was an ideal base. Its ring of islets enclosed the world's largest lagoon. There were airfields at the twin islets of Roi-Namur in the north, and Kwajalein Islet in the south. Howlin' Mad Smith chose a Marine division to seize Roi-Namur and an Army division to take Kwajalein.

Long before the assaults began on February 1, 1944, the Americans hurled enormous aerial raids at these objectives. They were determined not to repeat the

At the command, Marines scramble out of their hastily dug trench to take a Japanese position on Tarawa.

mistakes of Tarawa. The Navy also made sure that its bombardment would be more effective. They had trained a special force of bombardment ships—mainly the refitted old battlewagons sunk at Pearl Harbor—and developed a shore-sea spotting system which could pinpoint the targets. Before the invasions began, this bombardment force was battering away. During the shelling, Rear Admiral Richard Conolly earned his nickname of "Close-in Conolly." Watching the *Maryland* off Roi-Namur, he noticed she had not hit the blockhouses. He radioed: "Move really close in."

This time the transports were sent inside the lagoons, instead of standing outside as at Tarawa. And before the assault waves of amtracs roared shoreward, little islands to the sides of the objectives were taken as artillery sites.

When the Marines finally landed at

127

Roi, they came upon a scene of ruin and desolation. Hundreds of dead enemy soldiers lay sprawled over the shell-pocked airfield. Blockhouses lay on heaps of rubble. Japanese aircraft littered the airstrips like giant broken birds.

Roi fell easily to the Marines in a single day. But across the causeway, on the twin island of Namur, there was another sort of battle—a bitter one. It was called the Battle of the Drainage Ditches, because the Japanese lay hidden in long trenches and picked off the attacking Americans. During the night a Japanese counterattack was beaten off after a wild battle, and the next day the tanks led the Marine riflemen in a conquering sweep across the island.

Down to the south, American soldiers carried out a near-perfect waterborne assault on Kwajalein Islet. Eighty-four amtracs in four neat waves swept toward the beach, carrying men who had fought in the deep snowdrifts of Attu. Now the same soldiers were sailing over the white-capped lagoon toward a wrecked and smoking island on which an occasional nodding palm tree was still visible. They landed without casualty, but encountered heavy fighting inland. Half of the island's 5,000-man garrison was still alive. The American advance proved to be a toe-by-toe, shot-for-shot battle through a maze of pillboxes, antitank traps, and blockhouses. But Kwajalein Islet was taken in four days.

Now, with Kwajalein Atoll and its fine airfields and unsurpassed anchorage in his hands, Admiral Nimitz reached out for Eniwetok Atoll. This westernmost island-ring in the Marshalls was taken by a Marine regiment.

At Eniwetok, the *battleships* actually sailed inside the lagoon. They were a dreadful sight for the Japanese defenders to see: enormous steel monsters with swaying masts and towers and long spiky guns gliding right up to their shores. It was as though someone had poked a huge cannon in their front window.

Even after the dreadful bombardment, though, there were enough Japanese alive to kill Americans. Worse, the ground was sown with mines which exploded under thirty-five pounds of pressure. Many Marines were to die before, as one American lieutenant wrote, "We finally killed them all."

The Marshall Islands, taken from Germany and given to Japan after World War I, were now American bases for the remainder of World War II.

During the completion of the Marshalls conquests, Admiral Nimitz called upon the mighty United States Navy to knock out another enemy ocean fort —Truk. Called "The Gibraltar of the

Marines on Eniwetok await the word to attack. The fourth man down the line is carrying a flame thrower, used to dig out Japanese holed up in dugouts.

Pacific," Truk was Japan's powerful base in the heart of the enormous Caroline Islands chain. It was actually a drowned mountain range inside a coral reef. The wooded peaks sticking above vast Truk Lagoon were the islands on which Japanese airfields and supply dumps were located.

In the early days of the war American strategy planners blanched whenever someone mentioned taking Truk by direct assault. By early 1944, however, the Navy had many of the big fast flattops which were to prove so decisive in the war. Powerful new battleships were also plentiful. Therefore in mid-February, almost simultaneous with the Eniwetok assault, a combined striking force of warships and carriers raced up to Truk and struck hard.

Aircraft pounced with a sudden roar on Truk's airfields and shot up parked Japanese planes. Avengers skimmed low over the lagoon loosing specially rigged torpedoes. Mighty *New Jersey* and *Iowa* led a battle force around the atoll on the lookout for escaping ships. For two days the assault raged, and when it was over the Gibraltar of the Pacific had been reduced to smoking rubble. Japan lost 200,000 tons of merchant shipping, 275 airplanes, one cruiser, and three destroyers. The destruction was so complete that Nimitz could afford to by-pass Truk without landing any troops. American sea power was now clearly the mightiest the world had ever seen, and Admiral Nimitz was free to turn to the very heart of Japan's island barrier.

The Marianas Islands were to Japan what Pearl Harbor was to America. Their loss would uncover the island empire's inner defenses. The big Marianas islands of Saipan, Tinian, and Guam could be made into American bases for the huge new B-29 Superfort bombers just coming into production. Thus Japan would be brought within bombing range. Also, a Marianas invasion fleet might lure the Japanese fleet out into decisive battle.

Saipan was the first of the Marianas to be attacked.

On the morning of June 15, 1944, American warships sailed around the island with flaming guns. Marines of the two assault divisions churning ashore could see the peak of 1,500-foot Mount Topotchau piercing the black smoke clouds hanging over the island.

As at Tarawa, the Japanese had their guns zeroed in on the landing beaches. They even had colored flags in the water marking the range for masses of artillery on the high ground overlooking the beachhead. But this time the Navy's Underwater Demolition Teams, or frogmen, had systematically scouted and charted the reefs in advance of the landing. The Marines roared through the defensive fire, led by new amphibious tanks called "armored pigs." Landing, the men charged inland. In a few more days, an army division landed behind them. Soon the airfield in the south fell, and the three American divisions wheeled to begin a long, grinding battle toward the northern end of the island.

By then the Japanese fleet had bitten hard on the Saipan bait.

Fleet Admiral Soemu Toyoda had re-

Under enemy fire, Marines on the beach at Saipan crawl to their assigned positions. The wet Leatherneck (closest to camera) took a ducking when his landing craft was hit by Japanese mortar fire. In the background are armored "Buffalos."

placed Admiral Koga, who had died. Toyoda, as well as the Americans, wanted an all-out naval battle. He had expected it to come off New Guinea, where General MacArthur was launching new attacks. He did not expect it off the Marianas, and neither did the Japanese hero of Pearl Harbor—Admiral Chuichi Nagumo—who was trapped on Saipan when the Americans attacked.

The morning that Admiral Toyoda heard of the Saipan landings, he issued his orders:

"The Combined Fleet will attack the enemy in the Marianas area and annihilate the invasion force."

Five heavy carriers, four light carriers, and five battleships under Ad-miral Jisaburo Ozawa began steaming east toward Saipan. Awaiting them was an even stronger American force: seven heavy carriers, eight light carriers, and seven battleships, under Admiral Raymond Spruance.

Admiral Spruance knew of the Japanese approach. His submarines had been shadowing Ozawa and reporting regularly. Unhurried, Spruance detached his carriers under Admiral Marc Mitscher and sent them racing west to intercept the enemy. In the meantime, he continued to guard Saipan with the remaining ships.

On June 19, 1944, the great Battle of the Philippine Sea began.

The very first blows—struck by American submarines—were shattering to Japan. *Albacore* fired a spread of six torpedos into *Taiho,* the carrier that was Admiral Ozawa's flagship, and she blew up late in the afternoon. Ozawa transferred to another carrier, but in the meantime the submarine *Cavalla* had fired three fish into mighty *Shokaku.* The Japanese flattop fell apart and sank after a bomb magazine exploded.

Overhead, American fliers were shooting down enemy planes at such a rapid rate that they nicknamed the action "The Marianas Turkey Shoot." Next day they sank another big carrier, *Hiyo,* along with a few lesser ships, and damaged others. On the night of June 20 Admiral Ozawa, who had begun the battle with 430 aircraft on his decks, made this entry in his log: "Surviving carrier air power: 35 aircraft operational." In all, Japan lost three big carriers and 476 airplanes of all types, while America lost 130 planes, with only three ships damaged. United States losses in aircraft would not have been half so great if the bold American fliers had not pursued the fleeing Ozawa during darkness. Eighty planes were lost because they could not find their carriers, or ran out of gas. But many were rescued. Whereas Japan lost 445 aviators, America lost only 76.

No nation had ever before been so badly beaten in the skies.

And on Saipan, during those late June days, the battered, grimy, and sun-blistered Americans drove grimly north through the Pacific War's worst artillery barrages. Early in July a terrible Banzai charge overran American positions, but

it was soon contained and turned into a Japanese slaughter. The Japanese army commander killed himself, and Admiral Nagumo followed suit. On July 10, Saipan fell.

Japan was staggered. Premier Tojo fell from power, and General Kuniaki Koiso formed a new cabinet. The Japanese began to see that there was no longer any hope of victory. Scores of Japanese civilians and soldiers on Saipan killed themselves in a misguided fear of American reprisals.

Guam was next.

The Americans wanted Guam for reasons of pride. This southern Marianas island had once been American, and Guam's fall would signal the first recapture of American territory.

On July 21 the Americans came back to Guam. A Marine division and brigade made the assault. As before, the landings were bitterly contested. And as had happened so frequently in the Pacific, the Japanese broke their own backs with another Banzai charge.

This was the biggest nighttime counterattack of the war, and it was also the most drunken. The Japanese commanders deliberately gave their men large quantities of wine to drink before they attacked. They worked them into a frenzy. Japanese soldiers outside the Marine lines began screaming, singing, laughing, smashing empty bottles, and clanging bayonets against rifle barrels. "The Emperor draws much blood tonight," they yelled, hoping to frighten the Marines. But they only gave away their position. When the Japanese finally attacked, Marine guns made a flashing, crashing, crackling slaughter among them. Although there was a breakthrough at one point in the Marine line, the enemy soldiers were rounded up and destroyed at daylight.

The Americans resumed the attack, moving through a litter of broken bottles and dead enemy soldiers. An Army division which had come ashore joined the up-island drive. These soldiers were the first to liberate the Chamorro population imprisoned by the Japanese. The Chamorros had been brutally treated for their loyalty to America, and some of them had been beheaded. They had received little food and no medical care. Clothed in rags, many of them looked like skeletons. But they laughed and sang patriotic songs. Tears fell from the eyes of their liberators to behold such fidelity.

On August 10, 1944, Guam was "secured." Old Glory flew once again in its rightful place.

By then the Stars and Stripes were also flying over the third Marianas island to be conquered—Tinian.

Tinian lay immediately south of Saipan, separated only by a narrow strait. The Japanese commanders thought they had all possible landing beaches so fortified that Tinian could not be taken. But Major General Harry Schmidt, with the assistance of some Marines and Navy frogmen, went scouting for undefended beaches.

Two were found at the northwest tip, just opposite Saipan. They were only about sixty yards and one hundred yards wide, scarcely roomy enough to receive twenty thousand men. But General Schmidt decided to deceive the enemy. He put one Marine division aboard troop transports and sent it south to make a feint at the defended beaches. Then, while the Japanese commanders rushed all their troops to that threatened point, he sent another Marine division pouring over the strait and streaming up the two narrow beaches on the northwest coast.

The trick worked.

Tinian became known as the masterpiece of amphibious warfare. The Japanese were so surprised they were never able to recover. Naval bombardment helped confuse them, and for the first time American aircraft used the new napalm bomb. This was a tank of jellied gasoline which burst upon contact and sent long splashes of flame streaming through the air. The bombs set Tinian's canefields on fire, thus holding up Japanese troop movements while so terrifying enemy soldiers that they refused to move to the true landing beaches.

Tinian fell in a week, on August 1, 1944. Less than three months later—on November 24—giant B-29s of the Army Air Forces rose from airfields on the Marianas Islands to stagger Tokyo with its first massive bombing raid. Aerial retribution was coming closer to the Axis partner in Asia.

It had already overtaken Germany.

Holding their rifles aloft, Marine assault troops wade toward the Tinian beach.

24 | Air War on Germany

In the early days of the war, Marshal Hermann Goering had been fond of boasting: "If a single bomb falls on Berlin you can call me Meyer!" By the middle of 1943 battered Berliners huddled nightly in their bomb shelters and wryly asked each other: "Where's Meyer?"

They meant Goering, of course, or more exactly the Luftwaffe. But the German air force had been blasted from the skies, and the German nation was suffering a terrible reprisal for the open bombing of cities begun by Adolf Hitler.

Such retaliation had begun over Cologne in May of 1942. Gradually the British Bomber Command struck deeper and deeper into the German heartland. The cities of the industrial Ruhr were brought under devastation. More and more flights of big Lancaster bombers thundered aloft from English airfields to fill the night air of Germany with their thundering. They followed different courses, but their flights were timed to arrive over the target together. German defenses were kept guessing, and British fighter flights helped confuse the enemy by feinting here and there to draw off interceptor strength.

By 1943 the Allies had perfected many devices which permitted bombing attacks in any kind of weather. In addition, the British had built bombers big enough to carry the new eight-ton "block-buster" bomb. On July 24 of that year the British began a week-long aerial assault upon the great German seaport of Hamburg. More than eight thousand tons of explosives were dropped. So many fire bombs fell one night that a "fire tornado" sprang up and rushed through the city with a dreadful howl.

Berlin was also bombed in 1943.

Scourged by night, the German people soon found themselves staggered by day under the mass precision-bombing of American Flying Fortresses. Even when flying high above the black puffs of German antiaircraft shells, the Americans were able to pinpoint their bombing with deadly accuracy. Massed together, heavily armed Flying Forts were able to beat off the German fighters rising to attack them.

On August 1, 1943, a daring raid was made against the vast oil fields at Ploesti in Rumania. American Liberator bombers flew 1,200 miles from bases in Africa. They had to fly to their destination without fighter escorts and then turn around and fly back. They came in at low-level altitude, through clouds of ack-ack from heavy antiaircraft defenses. Fifty-four out of one hundred and seventy-seven bombers failed to return, but they had destroyed forty per cent of Ploesti's oil fields. Some officers thought that the cost at Ploesti had been too high. And as 1943 turned into 1944, others said that new types of German

A B-24 bomber braves the strong German antiaircraft defenses to drop destruction on the oil fields of Ploesti.

fighters were beginning to shoot down too many Flying Forts.

Alarmed, General Henry H. ("Hap") Arnold wrote to his Air Force commanders: "This is a MUST. . . . Destroy the enemy Air Force. . . ."

New types of long-range fighter planes such as the Thunderbolts and Mustangs were put into action so that the bombers might have fighter escorts. Established Air Force heroes grew even more famous, and new ones were born. Colonel John C. Meyer shot down thirty-seven planes; Lieutenant Colonel Francis Gabreski got thirty-three, and the famous fighting twins—Captains Don S. Gentile and John T. Godfrey—downed thirty and thirty-six respectively. These

last two fought under Colonel Donald Blakeslee, who stayed in active combat longer than any other American pilot in the European Theater of Operations. And when Colonel Blakeslee led Mustang fighters right over Berlin to escort American bombers, the Berliners knew that Marshal Goering's name was Meyer for sure.

The climax of the aerial war against Germany came during February and March of 1944. Desperate, the Luftwaffe massed its fighter strength and hurled it into the skies. But the Americans were too strong and too skillful. Approximately eight hundred German planes were shot down, and the Luftwaffe ceased to be an effective air force.

Captains John Godfrey (left) and Don Gentile—the famous fighting twins.

By early 1944 the Allies were ready for the big push in Italy.

Until the end of 1943 the Germans in Italy had held off the thrusts of the United States Fifth and the British Eighth armies. The enemy stood firm in the position known as the Gustav Line. So the Allies decided to sail around the Nazi forces.

On January 22, 1944, under cover of American bombers, a British and an American division landed at the little west coast town of Anzio, thirty-three miles south of Rome. It was a surprise stroke and it caught the Germans unprepared. Even so, Marshal von Kesselring did not pull back from the Gustav Line to defend himself against the menace in his rear as the Allies had hoped. Instead he tried to drive the Anzio force back into the sea.

And he nearly succeeded.

Artillery was rushed to the heights surrounding the beachhead. Veteran German formations went racing out of reserve against the Anglo-American positions. Alarmed, the Allies fed in more and more troops, most of them American. Von Kesselring countered with fresh units of his own, for Hitler had ordered the Allied foothold destroyed.

Anzio became a terrible killing-ground.

Thousands of young German soldiers died beneath the very muzzles of American machine guns. They charged des-perately, and came so close to success that the Allies began to consider evacuation. But a brave American battalion broke the attack, suffering terrible casualties in doing so. More charges followed. German riflemen rode their tanks into battle, and American riflemen picked them off. Up in the hills, the Germans massed monster Tiger tanks to fire-and-move, fire-and-move. Tiny tanks stuffed with explosives and operated by remote control—"Goliaths," the Germans called them—came scuttling into American positions to explode with searing blasts. At night the Luftwaffe sent over "the popcorn man"—flights of small bombers which unloaded hundreds of deadly butterfly bombs.

Eventually the Allied hold on Anzio tightened, and the Americans burst out of the German stranglehold. When they had taken the high ground above the town, they looked back and wondered how they had managed to hold on.

They could count almost every house and tree in Anzio.

Because Anzio had not succeeded in turning the enemy's flank, the Allies decided that they would have to batter down the Gustav Line. The key point in this line was the famous and ancient monastery of Monte Cassino, founded in 529 by St. Benedict. Monte Casino's fame was worldwide. The abbey was sacred to Protestants and Catholics

Amphibious "Ducks" of the Fifth Army come ashore and move inland to help establish an Allied beachhead at Anzio.

alike, for it had been one of the citadels of culture and civilization during the Dark Ages.

To the Germans, the steep, rocky hillside crowned by the stone monastery at the top was an excellent military position. They fortified it, but they did not occupy the abbey itself.

Monte Cassino resisted all Allied attacks.

Sorrowfully, the Allied command decided that the abbey must be bombed. Leaflets were dropped in both the town of Cassino and the abbey grounds, declaring:

"We have until now been careful to avoid bombarding Monte Cassino. The Germans have taken advantage of this. The battle is now closing in more and more around the sacred precincts. Against our will we are now obliged to direct our weapons against the Monastery itself. We warn you so that you may save yourselves. Leave the Monastery at once. This warning is urgent. It is given for your good."

On February 15, 1944, a force of 254 American bombers dropped 576 tons of explosives on the ancient abbey. In jets of flame, in a sudden spurt of smoke rising five hundred feet high, the cathedral and its cloisters collapsed in heaps of rubble.

Still the Germans fought on. New Zealanders attacking into the shambles found that the Allied bombardment, like the German devastation of Stalingrad, had spread a camouflage coating of rubble over and around ditches, cellars, craters, sewers, and fragments of buildings. Everywhere German riflemen and machine gunners lay concealed behind these ruins. A deadly game of hide-and-seek developed.

In March, the town of Cassino was bombed, this time by 500 American aircraft unloading 1,400 tons of bombs. But as so often happens when an already flattened position is bombed from the air, this great outpouring of destruction merely shook the rubble.

Not until May 18 was Monte Cassino in Allied hands. By then a great Allied spring offensive launched on May 11-12 had finally burst the Gustav Line on both coasts.

The Americans broke out of Anzio and clattered up the road to Rome. Much of the hardest fighting in this offensive was done by the Polish divisions. An unknown poet has written their epitaph on the memorial in their cemetery. It says:

> *We Polish soldiers*
> *For our freedom and yours*
> *Have given our souls to God*
> *Our bodies to the soil of Italy*
> *And our hearts to Poland.*

The devastated abbey at Monte Cassino.

The freedom for which these gallant men died was soon to come to the mother city of Western civilization: Rome.

On June 3 the Americans knocked down the last of the German defenses outside the city, and the next day they entered Rome in triumph. Cheering throngs sang songs and hurled flowers at the grimy liberators moving through the streets on foot with slung rifles, or standing upright in the jeeps and tanks and trucks that flowed steadily into the heart of the city.

The sun of liberty shone once again in the Eternal City.

Two days later it came back to the shores of France.

American armored vehicles rumble past the ancient Colosseum as the Allies occupy Rome.

26 | Invasion of Europe

You will enter the Continent of Europe and, in conjunction with the other United Nations, undertake operations aimed at the heart of Germany and the destruction of her armed forces.

This was the order for the invasion of Europe given by the Combined Chiefs of Staff to General Eisenhower, Supreme Commander, Allied Expeditionary Forces. To carry it out, Ike had assembled the mightiest striking force yet seen in the history of warfare. Southern England became a bristling armed camp. No less than 1,627,000 American soldiers and 53,000 sailors were quartered there. Marching soldiers clogged the roads. The air was full of the sound of rifles crackling or of the boom of cannon as Allied soldiers tested their weapons. The masts of hundreds of ships made the harbors look like watery forests. Docks were heaped high with supplies.

Everything was needed for this invasion: not only tanks and trucks and grenades and medical supplies, but railroad locomotives, newly minted French money, bulldozers, every kind of landing craft imaginable, entire telephone exchanges, power plants, radio stations, buses, hospitals, prison cages and police stations, bakeries and laundries, to say nothing of huge supplies of ammunition, food, clothing, and gasoline.

There were even portable ports!

These were called Mulberries. They were enormous concrete structures looking like six-story buildings lying on their sides. Two of them were built to be towed across the Channel and sunk opposite the invasion beaches, where they were to serve as sheltered docks in which ships could unload in any kind of weather. There were also groups of old ships which were to be towed off the beaches and then sunk stem-to-stern to form breakwaters.

Such were some of the provisions for this enormous assault, and they have never been equaled before or since.

During the last ten days of preparation, a ten-mile strip of southern England was declared off-limits to the average Englishman. All exits from England to other countries were sealed off. Mail from American servicemen to the United States was held up for ten days.

"The mighty host was tense as a coiled spring," General Eisenhower said. "And indeed that is exactly what it was —a great human spring, coiled for the moment when its energy should be released and it would vault the English Channel in the greatest amphibious assault ever attempted."

For the invasion alone Ike had gathered 150,000 men, 1,500 tanks, 2,727 ships and small craft, and 12,000 planes. But before this juggernaut of men and arms was hurled at the coast of Normandy, or northern France, the invasion area itself had to be sealed off.

Allied air power rose thundering to the challenge. German coastal defenses were flattened. Road and rail networks were wrecked. The French were warned to stay out of the danger area, while the French Underground was alerted to spring to arms on D-Day, the invasion date. Finally, the German commander in France, Marshal Gerd von Rundstedt, was tricked into expecting the invasion in the wrong place.

General Eisenhower chose to land in Normandy because he knew von Rundstedt expected him to cross the Channel over the narrow Dover-to-Calais route. Von Rundstedt had about nineteen divisions in the Calais area. Ike wanted to keep them there. So an elaborate dummy "Headquarters" was built in Dover. Divisions not to be used in the first days of the invasion were quartered in Dover. Details of a "Calais invasion" were deliberately leaked to known German agents. For every scouting mission flown over Normandy, one was flown over Calais. The Calais area was bombed nearly as heavily as Normandy.

The deception worked. Even after the landings in Normandy began, von Rundstedt held fast with his Calais divisions, confident that Normandy was merely a feint to draw him off.

Meanwhile, the Desert Fox had come to France to command the Atlantic Wall. Marshal Rommel had decided that the Allies must be stopped at the water's edge. "The enemy must be annihilated before he reaches our main battlefield,"

he told his officers. To do this, he began sowing in French coastal waters a deadly garden of mine fields, barbed wire, dragon's teeth, hedgehogs, and other obstacles. Unluckily he also took note of that neglected stretch of Normandy coast on which the Anglo-American forces intended to land. He packed all his forward troops and guns up to the water's edge and brought his reserves forward. "Believe me, Lang," Rommel told his aide, "the first twenty-four hours of the invasion will be decisive . . . the fate of Germany depends on the outcome. For Germany, it will be the longest day."

That day—or D-Day as it is called—was dictated by the weather. The tides had to be right for the boats to get ashore, and there had to be a full moon the preceding night when the paratroopers were to jump. Only a few days in June fulfilled these conditions. General Eisenhower chose the morning of June 5, 1944.

Then the weather turned against the Allies.

On June 4 grim, gray clouds drifted low over Normandy. High winds and mountainous waves buffeted the beaches. In such weather, the small landing boats would founder. Worse, there could be no air cover. Ike postponed the invasion, calling back the ships that were already on their way.

At half-past three in the morning of June 5, 1944, Ike and his generals were gathered in conference again. A hurricane wind howled about their headquarters. Faces were grave. Captain

Protected from enemy air attack by barrage balloons, the Allied invasion fleet crosses the English Channel.

Yank paratroopers, heavily armed, soar over the Channel to jump into France.

J. M. Stagg, chief weatherman, began speaking directly to Ike.

"I think we have found a gleam of hope for you, sir. The mass of weather fronts coming in from the Atlantic is moving faster than we anticipated. We predict there will be rather fair conditions beginning late on June 5 and lasting until the next morning, June 6, with a drop in wind velocity and some break in the clouds."

A silence lasting fully five minutes came upon the conference. General Eisenhower sat on a sofa in front of a bookcase. His face was tense and grave. The decision was all his: should he risk a change in the weather as predicted, or order a month's delay which could only help the Germans? Ike looked up. His face was calm.

"Okay," he said, "we'll go." June 6, 1944, would be D-Day.

The night of June 5, the great gray shapes of the ships began standing out to sea. They carried five assault divisions. One Canadian and two British were to land at three beaches—named Sword, Juno, and Gold—on the left; two American divisions would hit Omaha and Utah Beaches on the right.

Even as these ships sailed, airplanes thundered overhead carrying one British and two American airborne divisions to battle. These men were to jump behind German lines to seal off the beachhead. They roared over France. By the pale light of a rising moon, men in battle dress and jumping harness could see farms and fields below them. Over the jump areas, many of the transports plunged into murky clouds. And then came cries from the jump masters stationed at open doors:

"Let's go!"

They leaped, falling through billowing mists or moonlit skies. Many of them fell in swamps. Weighted by weapons and caught in their parachute harness, they drowned in three feet of water. Some of them broke their limbs as they fell. Lieutenant Colonel Benjamin Vandervoort broke his ankle, but the medics who jumped into action with him rigged him a stirrup-crutch and cut him a stick for a cane. Vandervoort fought the entire campaign on his broken ankle.

Many paratroopers were shot down as they drifted through the air, or were taken prisoner after they landed. Gradually, however, the others joined forces. The Americans had dime-store crickets which they used for signaling. One squeeze, *click-clack,* was answered by two, *click-clack click-clack.* Growing in force, the paratroops knocked out guns and seized the causeways through a wide lagoon behind the American beaches. This was important. If the enemy held those causeways, the American troops would never be able to burst out of their beachheads.

And with the dawn of D-Day the beachheads were blazing with battle.

A thousand British bombers had plastered the German defenses during the night. Another thousand American bombers struck at daylight. Thousands and thousands more flew air cover over the channel or strafed the beaches. Six big American and British battleships

145

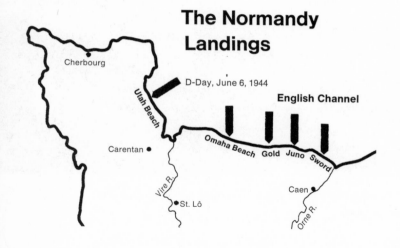

The Normandy Landings

Cherbourg

D-Day, June 6, 1944

English Channel

Utah Beach

Carentan

Omaha Beach Gold Juno Sword

Vire R.

St. Lô

Caen

Orne R.

The assault boats were taking hits, but still they came on. In one of the British boats a major read his men passages from Shakespeare's *King Henry V*, which tells of a British invasion of France in 1415.

> *And gentlemen in England*
> *   now abed,*
> *Shall think themselves accurs'd*
> *   they were not here.*

Aboard the American craft, the crouching, helmeted Yanks grasped their rifles and shouted to each other above the roar of the engines.

Out on the cruiser *Augusta,* long-jawed General Omar Bradley was worried. He had heard that the "DD" tanks rigged to "swim" ashore were sinking. This valuable weapon, on which the generals had relied heavily, was turning out to be of almost no use. The battle was now up to the foot soldier, protected by a cotton jacket and wielding a hand gun.

The fighting was raging fiercely on all the beaches. Yanks, "Canucks," and Tommies had waded ashore. They were struck by storms of carefully aimed fire. On Sword, Juno, and Gold, the Germans were resisting with their customary doggedness and skill.

On Utah Beach on the far right, resistance was not so heavy—except in the case of a unit of 200 Rangers given the dangerous mission of seizing a 100-foot cliff. The Rangers were shot at while still on the sea, and fifteen of them were hit as they ran ashore. They set up mortars. From these they fired

stood well out to duel with the German coastal batteries. Destroyers swarmed inshore to pepper German pillboxes. Rocket ships loosed their swooshing missiles like flights of giant' arrows. Minesweepers cleared the offshore depths, while frogmen in green-rubber suits leaped into closer waters to blow up obstacles and clear the way for the assault boats.

In they came.

The Germans recovered from the shock of the bombardment and began shooting back. Most of the American bombs had fallen harmlessly in hedgerows three miles inland. On some beaches not more than twenty per cent of the defense fortifications had been knocked out. German artillery began baying. Mortars whuffled into the sky, machine guns stuttered, antiboat guns whanged, pillboxes boomed orange flame, and the little Goliath tanks whizzed out to the beaches to greet the invaders with a shattering roar.

Smoke streams from a landing craft approaching the French coast. German machine-gun fire has just set off an American soldier's hand grenade.

ropes and rope ladders fitted with grapnel hooks onto the clifftop. About a dozen of the hooks caught. The Rangers began climbing. The Germans shot down the leading men. They cut the ropes. An American destroyer swept inshore and fired at the Germans. The Rangers kept on climbing, hand over hand. They reached the top of the cliff. It was empty. They pushed inland, shooting Germans, and found the guns. They blew up the breeches of the mighty weapons. Now the German artillery could not strike at Americans on Omaha.

But something worse awaited the Americans on Omaha. A first-rate German division happened to be on maneuvers on the bluffs above Omaha at the time of the attack. Its units were rushed into the breach. They poured a terrible killing fire on the Americans below them.

At half-past six the spearhead company had approached the beach in six landing craft. One of them sank and another was sunk by shellfire. The other four halted at a sand bar. The landing ramp came down, and the men leaped into water that was waist to shoulder deep. Here is that company's own story:

"As if this were the signal for which the enemy had waited, all boats came under criss-cross machine-gun fire. . . . As the first men jumped, they crumpled and flopped into the water. Then order was lost. It seemed to the men that the

General Omar Bradley

only way to get ashore was to dive head first in and swim clear of the fire that was striking the boats. But, as they hit the water, their heavy equipment dragged them down and soon they were struggling to keep afloat. Some were hit in the water and wounded. Some drowned then and there . . . But some moved safely through the bullet-fire to the sand and then, finding they could not hold there, went back into the water and used it as cover, only their heads sticking out. Those who survived kept moving forward with the tide, sheltering at times behind under-water obstacles and in this way they finally made their landings.

"Within ten minutes of the ramps being lowered, A Company had become inert, leaderless and almost incapable of action. Every officer and sergeant had been killed or wounded. . . . It had become a struggle for survival and rescue. The men in the water pushed wounded men ashore ahead of them, and those who had reached the sands crawled back into the water pulling others to land to save them from drowning, in many cases only to see the rescued men wounded again or to be hit themselves. Within 20 minutes of striking the beach A Company had ceased to be an assault company and had become a forlorn little rescue party bent upon survival and the saving of lives."

Soon another company joined this agony. They were riddled at the water's edge. But elsewhere on Omaha soldiers were being landed under cover of smoke or in gaps in the enemy's field of fire. At one point they joined to beat back an enemy counterattack that might have hurled the Americans into the sea. In some places brave bands of Americans had run the 700-yard gantlet of enemy fire and gained the protection of the base of the bluffs. But on one beach an entire battalion lay under the cover

German-constructed steel and concrete obstacles offer inadequate cover for invading Allied troops.

of a sea wall. Its men were dazed and bewildered. No one moved or attempted to get through the barbed wire blocking their way inland.

A lieutenant and a wounded sergeant stood up, heedless of the enemy fire. The lieutenant looked down at the men huddled in the shingle behind the sea wall.

"Are you going to lie there and get killed, or get up and do something about it?" he asked.

The men looked at him with dazed eyes. The lieutenant and the sergeant turned and blew up the wire obstacles themselves. Inspired by this action, the men rose and ran inland. They picked their way cautiously through deadly mine fields. Wounded men lay where they fell, fearing to move lest they set off a mine. The others stepped over them, following the lieutenant on this tightrope walk with death, under fire all the way.

A platoon got through, then a company, soon a battalion. They split off into bands and fell upon the German gun positions menacing the beaches. They knocked them out, one by one.

That was how Omaha Beach finally fell to the Americans. The opening German fire had broken up the larger units. After the first dreadful shock—either of being blown into the water or of being pinned down under a ferocious fire—the soldiers began rallying individually or in small units. Under command of sergeants or junior officers they had risen to the attack. At first, one or two successes did not seem to mean much. But they grew in volume as the day wore on until the crack German division

A first-wave beach battalion takes advantage of a lull in enemy firing.

opposing the landing was all but destroyed. By nine o'clock in the morning there were Americans climbing Omaha's bluffs, and four hours later a much-relieved General Bradley received the delayed message:

"Troops formerly pinned down on beaches [are] advancing up the heights behind the beaches."

To the right of Omaha, the Rangers and soldiers on Utah had joined up and were steadily pressing the enemy backward.

To the left of Omaha, General Montgomery's divisions—not so stubbornly opposed—were driving inland and reaching penetrations as much as seven miles deep.

The Anglo-American invaders had their desired foothold. All day long the soldiers fought to expand it, while from the ship-choked channel behind them a torrent of supplies and reserve troops was flowing across the beaches.

D-Day was a great victory. Marshal Rommel's predicted "longest day" had ended in a German nightmare.

27 | France Free Again

Marshal Erwin Rommel had wisely predicted that the first twenty-four hours would be decisive, but unfortunately he was not present to lead his men during those crucial hours. After the weather had turned so foul on June 4, he recalled that the Allies had always before invaded in fair weather. So he thought it was safe to go home to Germany to help his wife celebrate her birthday.

As soon as he was informed of the invasion, he turned and hurried back to the front. But he was twenty-four decisive hours too late.

Rommel was not the only commander absent from his post that fateful sixth day of June. A half-dozen German generals had gone inland from the coast to take part in a "war game" based on a possible Allied landing in France! And the two Panzer divisions which might have ground the invaders into the beaches could not be used without Hitler's permission. The Fuehrer was asleep, and no one dared wake him. In fact, Hitler did not hear the full details of the invasion until mid-afternoon, and then he brushed it off as a raid. He calmly ordered von Rundstedt to squelch it, and turned to "more important" matters such as his new "wonder weapons."

These were robot bombs with which Hitler intended to snatch victory from defeat. The first of these robot bombs were launched at London a week after

D-Day. They were small, pilotless, jet-propelled bombs which the British nicknamed "buzz bombs" or "doodle-bugs." They were a new form of aerial terror, but not as dreaded as the terrible V-2 rockets which Hitler was to hurl at London three months later. The latter carried a ton of explosives and flew at supersonic speeds. They could not be heard or seen. The only warning was the explosion. V-2 rockets killed nearly as many Londoners as were killed in the famous blitz during the autumn of 1940.

There were launching sites for robot bombs in the Calais region where von Rundstedt expected the invasion to come. These sites had to be defended, and that was another reason why the German commander was reluctant to move south in force. It was mid-June before he realized that the true invasion had been in Normandy.

By then it was too late.

By June 10, the Allies had broken the Atlantic Wall for good. They held a solid eighty-mile stretch of the Normandy coast and had gone inland twenty miles. By June 12, nearly 90,000 vehicles and 600,000 men had been put ashore. On June 21 there were a million men.

Hitler was infuriated. He spoke curtly to Rommel, the commander he had so admired and elevated to an important rank. Again the Fuehrer ordered von Rundstedt to throw the invaders into the sea, as though it could be done as easily as it was said. "It is forbidden to shorten the front," Hitler raged. "It is not permitted to maneuver freely."

For a time such stand-fast tactics actually penned up the Allied advance. In the north General Montgomery had hoped to draw off German strength so that General Bradley's forces in the south might break out into open country. But Monty had never anticipated the blows that were bringing his armor to a halt above the key city of Caen.

In the south, the Americans were fighting the bloody "Battle of the Hedgerows." The fields were plotted and pieced in tiny lots by dense and heavy hedges that were centuries old. The hedges grew out of banks of earth three and four feet high. Sometimes there were double rows, forming a natural trench between them. Enemy riflemen, machine gunners, and antitank teams could lie hidden and protected inside the hedgerows. They massacred approaching infantrymen. American tanks could not butt through the hedges, because they had to climb the earthbanks. They rose almost vertically with guns uselessly pointed skyward and their soft underbellies exposed to any kind of antitank missile.

In the hedgerows, advances were measured in yards and bought dearly in blood. Finally an ingenious sergeant named Culin invented the "Rhinoceros tank," by fitting scythelike blades of steel to a tank's snout. The tank rammed the earthbank on an even keel with all guns firing, cut through it, and rumbled on its way covered by a camouflage of hedge. Then General Bradley

trained his troops in tank-infantry teamwork. And squadrons of Thunderbolt fighters were taught how to coöperate with the ground troops. Whenever the armor was balked by a roadblock, the Thunderbolts were notified by radio. The target was marked by smoke bombs, and the Yank fighters roared down to bomb and strafe. With the Rhino-tank and these new tactics, Bradley's First Army gradually slashed through the hedgerows.

On July 17 the shrewd brain behind the German defenses was removed permanently from the war. An American airplane caught Marshal Rommel's command car on the open highway and fired a cannon shell into it. Rommel was seriously injured. But soon the Desert Fox was to be in even greater trouble.

Sgt. Curtis Culin, ingenious inventor of the "Rhinoceros tank."

A "Rhino tank" rams its way through a French hedgerow.

For some time a plot had been hatching against Hitler's life. Many German officers were appalled by the crimes of the Nazis. They wanted to rescue German honor. They realized now that they could never beat the Allies, and they wanted to end the terrible retribution being visited on Germany from the skies.

On July 20, 1944, a German colonel, Count Klaus Schenk von Stauffenberg, arrived by plane at Hitler's headquarters in Rastenburg. This 37-year-old nobleman was a man of great personal charm and courage. He had been horribly wounded in Tunisia, losing his left eye, right hand, two fingers of his left hand, and much of the muscle power in his legs.

Count von Stauffenberg had a time bomb in his brief case. He carried the case right into the heavily guarded Wolf's Lair, where Hitler was holding a meeting with his generals. Placing the brief case under the table near Hitler, von Stauffenberg hurriedly made an excuse and left the room. He bluffed his way past the guards and drove to the airport, where he caught a plane for Berlin. There he and his fellow conspirators were to seize power the moment news of Hitler's death was received. Then they would begin talking

This photograph of Hitler was taken less than an hour after the attempt on his life. He is holding his injured arm. Goering is on the Fuehrer's right.

peace with the Allies.

Meanwhile, inside the conference room, an officer stumbled over von Stauffenberg's brief case. He moved it to the other side of a great oaken support, away from Hitler.

At 12:42 P.M. the bomb exploded. There were three separate blasts—three deafening roars—and three spouts of yellow flame. The roof fell in; timbers crashed to the floor, and thick clouds of smoke swirled everywhere.

"Murder!" cried one of the stricken generals. "Where is the Fuehrer?"

Adolf Hitler was on the floor pinned beneath a falling beam. He had been saved by the table top and the oaken support between him and the bomb. His right arm was temporarily paralyzed, and his eardrums had been punctured. His hair and legs were scorched. But he was alive, though the bomb had killed four officers and wounded twenty others. In no time Hitler was vowing dire and cruel revenge.

Von Stauffenberg and his followers were rounded up and executed. The revolt had been unbelievably bungled.

As for Rommel, he was quickly linked to the plot; two of Hitler's men visited the wounded general in the hospital and politely but firmly suggested he commit suicide. Rommel took poison. He knew that otherwise he would be subjected to a much more horrible death.

Thus ended the plot of July 20, 1944. After it, Hitler became convinced of his destiny. No one dared oppose his will any longer. His madness, coupled with the Allied insistence on Unconditional Surrender, was to prolong the war.

Five days after the plot failed, the American forces broke into the open. A "carpet bombing" of unbelievable weight and fury cleared the way. General Fritz Bayerlein, commander of the famous Panzer Lehr Division, has described the awful onslaught:

"The planes kept coming over, as if on a conveyer belt, and the bomb carpets unrolled in great rectangles. My flak had hardly opened its mouth, when the batteries received direct hits which knocked out half the guns and silenced the rest. After an hour I had no communication with anybody, even by radio. By noon nothing was visible but dust and smoke. My front-lines looked like the face of the moon and at least 70 per cent of my troops were out of action—dead, wounded, crazed or numbed. All my forward tanks were knocked out, and the roads were practically impassable."

After this, the Americans began to roll. Driving their tanks and half-tracks along like broncos, the Yanks overwhelmed the astonished Germans in a swift, swarming assault that made the blitzkrieg look as outmoded as a horse and buggy.

And now General Patton was back in battle. Upright in his jeep, the General was constantly at the front—urging, shouting, commanding—driving his new Third Army forward in a pell-mell race into Brittany.

"Get going!" Patton told his generals. "Never mind your flanks, just get going. I'll see you up there in a few days." He himself was always "up there," inspiring his men or roaring angrily whenever he found a slowdown or traffic jam that might hold up his beloved, rampaging tanks.

Early in the breakout General Patton found an entire armored division stalled in front of a river. He asked the commander why he hadn't crossed, and the general replied that his staff was studying the river for a safe place to ford. "Why not take a look yourself?" Patton snapped. "I did, and I just waded across. That river is only two feet deep and its only defense is a pretty poor machine gunner who couldn't even hit me!" Embarrassed, the commander got his division rolling.

After the Third Army found an unguarded bridge leading into Brittany, the Yanks really rolled ahead. Fighters flew air cover over the bridge and antiaircraft guns guarded it from the ground. Officers stood on the other side waving men on, pointing to all the roads, shouting, "Keep going, keep going!" In three days General Patton fed seven divisions over that bridge—105,000 men and 15,000 vehicles—and they fanned out quickly to overrun the countryside. Even

Adolf Hitler could not conceal his grudging admiration for that feat of organization.

"Look at that crazy cowboy general," he grumbled.

It was then that Hitler decided to counterattack. He would cut the far-flung Americans in two by a knifelike drive to the coast. The blow was delivered in early August. It pushed some of General Bradley's units back. But it was also just what Bradley had been waiting for.

Hitler had pushed a whole German army into the Allied noose.

While the Germans were battering toward the coast, Montgomery's Canadian-British force in the north and Bradley's Americans in the south could join forces behind them. The Germans would be trapped.

Acting swiftly, General Bradley ordered his forces in the south to race north toward Caen. In the meantime, Monty was to quicken his drive south. Unfortunately, General Montgomery's formations were not able to move as quickly as the Americans. This left an escape exit for the Germans. Even so, the German divisions racing frantically east toward Paris were scourged from the air as they passed through the so-

U.S. infantrymen in a French village creep alongside the walls of battered buildings as they close in on an enemy strong point.

called "Falaise Gap." General Bayerlein has also described this ordeal:

"Towards 0200 we were getting to Argentan. The scene was as bright as day—what with fires and explosions. The little town was quaking under the ceaseless hail of bombs. We got as far as the southern outskirts; after that it was impossible to get any farther. The whole of Argentan was burning. We were in a witch's cauldron. Behind us the road was blocked too. We were trapped in a blazing town. Dust and smoke reduced visibility to nil. Sparks were flying about our vehicles. Smoldering beams and wrecked masonry blocked all roads. And still the enemy planes were hovering in the sky. Their flares flooded the burning houses with brilliant light. We could hardly breathe with the pungent smoke. We had to reconnoiter a way out on foot. Teams of engineers were working on the heavily damaged bridge over the Orne. At 0300 we succeeded in escaping from this fiery cage across the fields in the direction of Flers."

Even though more than a third of the German Seventh Army was able to escape the trap, the Falaise Gap became the greatest German disaster since Stalingrad. Roads were littered with dead soldiers and wrecked, blackened vehicles.

Then, on August 15, the Germans were rocked by a fresh blow.

Allied troops landed in southern France. The United States Seventh Army and parts of the French First Army hit French ports on the Mediterranean. They were commanded by General Patch, who had relieved General Vandegrift on Guadalcanal. Patch's objective was to drive north to join up with Allied armies even then racing east in pursuit of the backtracking Germans.

General Patton's Third Army was the first to cross the Seine River, by-passing Paris in its eagerness to penetrate this natural defensive barrier. But on August 19, the underground French Forces of the Interior leaped to arms against the German garrison in Paris. General Eisenhower quickly sent help. The famous French Second Armored Division under General Jacques LeClerc was given the honor of entering the city, and on August 25, 1944, General LeClerc announced the German surrender.

Winston Churchill had said repeatedly to Ike, "General, if by the coming winter you have . . . freed beautiful Paris from the hands of the enemy, I will assert the victory to be the greatest of modern times."

As it turned out, the French capital was free again before the end of summer!

Paris went delirious with joy. A deeply emotional welcome greeted General Charles de Gaulle walking on foot down the center of the Champs Elysées. Throughout the long black night of the French occupation, he had upheld her honor.

Then the Parisians went wild over the Americans coming into the city. They mobbed them in a demonstration that reached its climax when generals de Gaulle and Bradley reviewed French and American troops marching past the

Surrounded by joyful Parisians, General de Gaulle walks down the Champs Elysées.

Arc de Triomphe. But this was no mere show-off parade. The troops were in full battle dress, passing through Paris on their way to the front.

Four huge spearheads were already thrusting through eastern France and Belgium. In speed and skill and strength they surpassed the Nazi drive against the Allies in the first Battle of France. By September 5—three months after D-Day —General Eisenhower had landed two million men and three and a half million tons of supplies in France. But the spearheads ate up gasoline and bullets like hungry monsters of war. Soon a "Red Ball Express" was organized to rush supplies east. It was a huge, circular, one-way trucking system running from Normandy to the front and back. Eventually the capture of the great Belgian port of Antwerp and its approaches brought supply centers closer to the front.

In early September of 1944 the British army slowed to a standstill on the Belgian-Dutch frontier. Three rivers— the Meuse, the Waal, and the Lower Rhine—blocked their way.

General Montgomery proposed an airborne operation into Holland. Its objective was to seize the heavily guarded bridges over the rivers and open a direct path into the German heartland. By this lightning thrust the Allies hoped to outflank the heavily fortified Siegfried Line and bring the war to a speedier conclusion.

Twenty thousand glider troops and paratroopers—from one British and two United States airborne divisions—were dropped on September 17. At first things went well. At Eindhoven and Nijmegen the American paratroops managed to seize the bridges after a hard fight, and ground troops came to their relief in time.

157

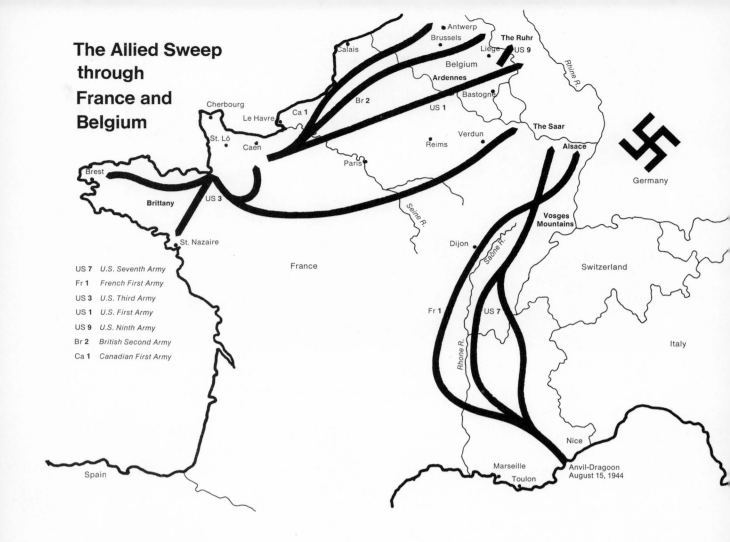

The Allied Sweep through France and Belgium

US 7   *U.S. Seventh Army*
Fr 1   *French First Army*
US 3   *U.S. Third Army*
US 1   *U.S. First Army*
US 9   *U.S. Ninth Army*
Br 2   *British Second Army*
Ca 1   *Canadian First Army*

But farther north a force of about 8,000 British airborne "Red Devils," so named for the bright red berets they wore, went through a dreadful nine-day ordeal. Their mission was to capture the Rhine bridge at Arnhem. Ground troops were to fight their way through to relieve them. But the Germans struck back so savagely that the infantry could not get through. The valiant Red Devils were sliced up into small groups and chopped to pieces. They hung on heroically. But in the end, when they had to be evacuated, there were only two thousand of them left.

So ended the heave across France into the shadow of the German Siegfried Line. Although the lightning blow had failed, the Allied armies under General Eisenhower had made a brilliant showing in the three and a half months that followed D-Day. After the setback at Arnhem, Eisenhower could not immediately try to enter Germany again, for winter was coming and the Allied armies had outrun their supplies.

U.S. paratroops float toward the earth in the invasion of Holland.

28 | The Polish Uprising

While the Second Front was being opened in the west, the Russians on the Eastern Front had been engaged in hurling the Germans from Russian soil.

Throughout winter, spring, summer, and fall of 1944, the Russians pursued their retreating enemy. They swept from river to river, city to city, in relentless, furious assault. The Soviet army was like a boxer scenting the kill, driving his opponent before him in a flurry of blows until he could corner him and knock him out.

One by one, captured Russian cities were torn from the invader's hand. Russian armed might stood again on the borders of the Baltic States. Unhappy Finland was once more invested by a Russian army, but this time by one far superior to the blundering horde that floundered in the snows of December, 1939. By early summer the Germans had been pushed back into Poland and Rumania.

In mid-July the Russians crossed the Vistula River in Poland. The sound of their guns could be heard in Warsaw. Russian bombs fell on the German garrison there.

Springing to arms, the patriots of Warsaw rose in revolt.

They had been urged to rise by the Moscow radio. They had enough food and ammunition for about a week, but they counted on help from the Red Army. Already, on July 31, the Russian divisions were within ten miles of the city and Red tanks were probing the suburbs. Next day, forty thousand men of the Polish Underground under General Tadeusz Bor-Komorowski turned on the German garrison.

"At exactly five o'clock thousands of windows flashed as they were flung open," General Bor-Komorowski reported. "From all sides a hail of bullets struck passing Germans, riddling their buildings and their marching formations. In the twinkling of an eye the remaining civilians disappeared from the streets. From the entrances of houses our men streamed out and rushed to the attack. In fifteen minutes an entire city of a million inhabitants was engulfed in the fight."

The Germans threw five full divisions into the battle. Three more—including the veteran Hermann Goering Division—were rushed to Poland from Italy. Alarmed, the Polish Government-in-Exile appealed for aid from the Allies. Britain rushed supplies by air. Prime Minister Churchill telegraphed Premier Stalin beseeching him to come to the rescue of the Polish Underground. So did President Roosevelt later on.

But Joseph Stalin had other plans for Poland. In the Polish Underground were many patriots who were as anti-Communist as they were anti-Nazi. Once the war was over, they would oppose the hand-picked Polish Communists whom Stalin was planning to place in power. But if these patriots were killed in the uprising they would be safely out of the way, and they would also serve the Red Army by killing thousands of Germans. So Premier Stalin rejected the pleas of his partners, Churchill and Roosevelt. He called General Bor's men "criminals."

The Red Army outside Warsaw waited.

Inside the blazing city, Poles and Germans were locked in a street-by-street struggle that must have been, for sheer savagery, one of the most violent in history. German tanks sometimes drove hundreds of Polish women and children in front of them as a shield against Polish troops. And the Polish Underground was literally fighting an underground war. The only means of communication between the Polish sectors was through the sewers. Germans threw grenades into these and sometimes jumped through manhole covers to give battle. Fights to the death took place between men standing waist deep in filth. Men perished by the knife or were drowned in slime.

Gradually, the overwhelming German weight of numbers and weapons pressed the valiant Poles to the ground. After two months of battle, the last message from Warsaw said:

"This is the stark truth. We were treated worse than Hitler's satellites, worse than Italy, Rumania, Finland. May God, who is just, pass judgment on the terrible injustice suffered by the Polish nation, and may He punish accordingly all those who are guilty.

Soviet machine gunners fire at the opposite bank of the Vistula River, driving the Germans out of their entrenchments.

"Your heroes are the soldiers whose only weapons against tanks, planes, and guns were their revolvers and bottles filled with gasoline. Your heroes are the women who tended the wounded and carried messages under fire, who cooked in bombed and ruined cellars to feed children and adults, and who soothed and comforted the dying.

"Immortal is the nation that can muster such universal heroism. For those who have died have conquered, and those who live on will fight on, will conquer and again bear witness that Poland lives while the Poles live."

Sadly, a new tyranny was to enslave the Poles. A few months after General Bor-Komorowski surrendered, Premier Stalin met Prime Minister Churchill and President Roosevelt at Yalta in Russia. Agreements were made there that eventually enabled Soviet Russia to draw the

161

states of Eastern Europe behind Communism's "Iron Curtain." Gradually Poland, Rumania, Bulgaria, Hungary, Czechoslovakia, and Yugoslavia were drawn into the Communist orbit. And the promises which Stalin made with regard to free elections in Poland were not kept.

Polish patriots who died fighting Nazis might have lived to oppose the Communists. But when the Soviet army entered Warsaw at the end of 1944, the unburied bodies of these patriots still lay in the streets.

That was "liberation" in communist style. But across the world at about the same time a true, heart-warming liberation took place in the Philippines.

Remnants of the heroic Polish Home Army, who surrendered only when all supplies were exhausted.

General MacArthur intended to return to the Philippines in November of 1944. But before he could do this, he had to have more bases in New Guinea and among the Japanese islands.

In late May of 1944, he began leapfrogging up the New Guinea coast again. He did this at the same time General Eisenhower was assembling history's mightiest invasion force for the cross-Channel invasion, and while Admiral Nimitz was putting together his vast armada for assaulting the Marianas. The coincidence of these three great operations proved beyond doubt that the United States had become the most powerful nation on earth. Only America was fighting a true two-ocean war: on land, in the air, and on the sea.

Biak and Noemfor were the most important New Guinea coastal islands taken by General "Mac." There wasn't much fighting at Noemfor, but some of the soldiers who captured it sailed seven hundred miles in open boats to the battleground.

At Biak, for the first time, the Japanese did not try to stop the Americans at the water's edge.

Instead, they "holed up." They contested every yard, almost every step. This was called "defense in depth." Because of it Biak was hard to conquer. But fall it did, and in September MacArthur reached for the final stepping stones to the Philippines.

These were the island of Morotai on the left and the island of Peleliu on the right. And then, even as MacArthur sailed with the soldiers who were to invade Morotai, there came electrifying news.

The Central Philippines were lightly defended.

Admiral Bull Halsey had led his Third Fleet up there and flown off his war birds at Samar. They sank many ships and shot up two hundred planes. In fact, they had things so much their own way that Halsey suggested that MacArthur change his plans. Instead of hitting the Southern Philippines in November as planned, he could smash right into the central island of Leyte in October.

MacArthur agreed.

Meanwhile, the General's soldiers landed on Morotai on September 15, 1944, against little opposition. But the Marines who hit Peleliu the same day ran into the bloodiest single-division battle of the war. The Japanese commander at Peleliu had perfected the defense tactics begun at Biak. And Peleliu was a natural fortress. Only six miles long and two miles wide, it was not really an island but an undersea coral reef heaved above the sea by a submarine volcano. As a result, it was pocked by caves. Some were just big enough for a sniper, some were big enough to hold a thousand men. Several of these caves were four and five levels deep. Others had sliding steel doors at their mouths. When the doors slid open, guns rolled out, fired, rolled back—and then the doors slid shut again.

Peleliu, then, was a hard, flinty coral reef filled with thousands of the Emperor's finest troops, all heavily armed and prepared to fight to the death.

The moment the Marines reached the outer reef the American bombardment lifted. From their amtracs, the men could not see Peleliu. It was hidden under a pink-glowing cloud of smoke. At the reef, the amtracs emerged from the sea with water streaming from their sides. They crossed the subsurface coral with the waddle of prehistoric monsters, then plunged back into the water and churned inland, only to be hit by a terrible enemy artillery fire.

Many boats sank and many men drowned. But most of them got ashore. Then the astonished Americans found that the Japanese had built underground burrows from position to position. If the Marines knocked out a pillbox and moved on, the position would be swiftly reoccupied and the enemy would begin

firing at them from the rear.

Then the Marines took the airfield, and the Japanese hurled a tank counterattack at them. The Americans knocked them all out. Most of the Japanese fell victim to airplanes swooping down low to launch wing rockets.

After the tank battle, the Marines moved into the heart of the enemy positions, a coral mountain known as "Bloody Nose Ridge." Inside their caves, the Japanese were cool. They had plenty of water. Outside, the Americans found themselves fighting in an oven. Temperatures rose to as high as 115 degrees. There was no escaping a brazen sun reflected off the naked coral. Men fainted of heat exhaustion. Salt tablets became as necessary at the front as blood plasma and bullets. The Marines pulled their camouflage cloths out of their helmets and let them hang over their blistering necks. They rarely saw the hidden enemy, although they themselves were constantly exposed. They had to clamber up the hillsides to fire into the cave mouths, shooting flame or hurling explosives inside them.

"Let's go get killed on that high ground up there!" a sergeant shouted to his men one day. And that was the dauntless spirit that finally took Peleliu, with the aid of an Army regiment rushed ashore to help the Marines. The island was officially "secured" on October 12. But even when its garrison was almost wiped out and its chief commanders dead of their own hands, isolated Japanese pockets of resistance continued to hold out. This was true on most of the Pacific islands.

On Peleliu a bulldozer tank fires at the mouth of a Japanese cave only 25 yards away. To the left of the tank is a Japanese 77-mm. gun previously knocked out.

On the morning of October 20, 1944, four divisions of American soldiers from Lieutenant General Walter Krueger's Sixth Army landed on Leyte.

Protecting them in the skies were the roaring aircraft of General George Kenney's Army Air Force. Patrolling the sea to their rear was the Seventh Fleet commanded by Vice Admiral Thomas C. Kinkaid. And to the north, ready to intercept the Japanese Combined Fleet if it appeared, was the enormous United States Third Fleet under Admiral William Halsey.

The Third Fleet had already struck hard at the Japanese. Its fliers had destroyed about 700 enemy airplanes in daring strikes at Formosa, Okinawa, and Luzon. The Japanese had pretended that this was not so. They broadcast boasts of having destroyed the Third Fleet. Bull Halsey's reply to that falsehood became famous. He signaled Admiral Nimitz:

"All Third Fleet ships reported by Tokyo as sunk have now been salvaged and are retiring at full speed in the direction of the enemy."

In such a mood of high-hearted confidence, MacArthur's soldiers came back to the Philippines. The surprised Japanese offered feeble resistance at first. Two beachheads were quickly seized, one just below Tacloban, the capital of Leyte, and another at Dulag.

A few hours after the assault troops hit the beaches, General MacArthur himself waded ashore. He stood atop an Army signal truck and publicly redeemed his pledge given two and a half years earlier.

"People of the Philippines: I have returned! By the grace of Almighty God our forces stand again on Philippine soil—soil consecrated in the blood of our two peoples."

Overjoyed, the Filipinos were quick to follow MacArthur's cry: "Rally to me."

In the skies over Leyte, the Japanese

General Douglas MacArthur (center) and a group of United States and Philippine army officers wade ashore at Leyte.

made a determined effort to sink the invasion fleet. For a few hours of October 24 they actually regained control of the air, losing it again under the daring attacks of Navy Hellcat pilots. One of these men, Commander David McCampbell, shot down nine enemy planes that day. He became the Navy's top ace with thirty-four kills.

Despite the initial success of the invasion, the American commanders were uneasy. Where was the enemy, they asked themselves, unaware that General Tomoyuki Yamashita was landing 45,000 men on Leyte's opposite coast. More mysterious: where was the Japanese navy?

It had come out to fight.

All that remained of Japan's mighty fleet—and there was still plenty left—was sailing with open muzzles toward the Philippines. The Battle of Leyte Gulf, which for sheer complexity and magnitude has never been equaled in naval history, was about to begin.

To the north of Leyte, Admiral Ozawa's four carriers sailed boldly back and forth. They were acting as bait for Bull Halsey. If the American took his Third Fleet north, Leyte would be defenseless from the sea. Then a Center Force under Admiral Takeo Kurita would slip through San Bernardino Strait and fall on the American light carriers. Destroying them, Kurita could chew up the transports and supply ships. So could a Southern Force of Japanese battleships and cruisers under Admiral Shoji Nishimura racing up through Surigao Strait.

The Americans would be dealt a blow that might turn the tide of the Pacific War.

At first, however, all the blows fell on the Japanese. The night of October 23 two American submarines, *Darter* and *Dace*, sighted Kurita's column of battleships and cruisers. At dawn, *Darter* attacked a Japanese cruiser and set her ablaze from stem to stern. *Dace* came up to periscope level, and her captain cried: "It looks like the Fourth of July out there!" Then *Dace* attacked and sank another cruiser.

Alerted by the submarines, Admiral Halsey hurled his carrier planes at Kurita. They sank a battleship and damaged other ships. Kurita turned around and sailed back the way he had come.

The Philippine Islands

To the south, Rear Admiral Jesse B. Oldendorf awaited the two Japanese battleships, four cruisers, and eight destroyers that Admiral Nishimura was leading up Surigao Strait. Oldendorf arranged his six battleships and eight cruisers in the classic battle line at the mouth of the Strait. His destroyers were put in front of the battle line, and thirty-nine torpedo boats went down the Strait on patrol duty.

A little after two o'clock in the morning Admiral Nishimura sailed into the trap.

Maneuvering brilliantly, the American destroyers hit the Japanese column from both sides. They broke up their formations, and by the time Nishimura's fleet reached Oldendorf's battle line, he had only one battleship, one cruiser, and one destroyer left. Then the giant American warships filled the night air with their bellowing. One Yankee captain said, "It was the most beautiful sight I have ever seen. The arched line of tracers in the darkness looked like a continual stream of lighted railroad cars going over a hill." Nishimura's battleship *Yamashiro* turned over and sank with the admiral aboard.

Then came the bad news.

Admiral Halsey had taken the Japanese bait. Believing that Admiral Kurita had been thoroughly beaten the day before, he had gone tearing north after Ozawa's force.

But Kurita had not been beaten. He had twenty-two ships left, including five battleships led by *Yamato*, the world's biggest. And he had sailed back through San Bernardino Strait and was steaming south toward the thin-skinned American invasion fleet.

Between Kurita and his prey stood nothing but three small baby-flattop task forces known as Taffy One, Taffy Two, and Taffy Three. Each of these formations included at least four of the small carriers with a few destroyers and destroyer escorts. Slow and lightly armed, the Taffy carriers matched against Kurita's battleships would be like rabbits fighting lions.

The moment Kurita's force was sighted, the Taffies flew off their planes to attack. Then they began making smoke and zigzagging in an effort to confuse the aim of the enemy gunners. The destroyers of Taffy Three headed directly toward the big enemy ships. One of these destroyers, *Heerman*, broke through the enemy screen and fought her way right up to *Yamato*, forcing the big battleship out of the battle temporarily by launching a spread of torpedoes. Another destroyer, *Johnston*, put a Japanese cruiser out of action with a single torpedo.

All of the American ships were taking hits. But the Japanese were firing huge armor-piercing shells that generally went right through the baby flattops' thin skins without exploding. *Ch-chung!* they would go, entering and leaving in almost the same instant. Nevertheless, the carrier *Gambier Bay* was sunk, as well as two destroyers and a smaller ship. The Japanese were gaining. It appeared that the plucky little carrier forces were doomed. Suddenly a lookout aboard *Fanshaw Bay* cried, "They're getting away!"

167

The plucky little Gambier Bay *is bracketed by shells from Admiral Kurita's Japanese fleet.*

Although the brave lookout's cry did not accurately describe what was happening—the careful withdrawal of Kurita's fleet—it certainly described the fighting spirit of the Taffies. Though outmaneuvered, the Yanks had not been outfought. The little carriers and their escorts had turned disaster into a bright victory. Nor were they content to sit and contemplate their victory. As soon as their planes could land and reload, they flew after Kurita's fleet again, damaging and destroying additional ships.

Moreover, Admiral Halsey in the north had succeeded in sinking four carriers, a cruiser, and three destroyers —certainly something the Japanese had not planned, even in offering "bait."

All told, the Japanese lost twenty-six of their warships, against six American vessels sunk.

The greatest naval battle of all time had ended in the ruination of the Japanese navy. Of course there were a few ships left, but not enough for the Japanese to undertake a major mission.

Ashore, the battle was not quite so easy. General Yamashita's men were fighting hard, and torrential rains had turned the roads into slops of mud. The engineers had trouble building airfields, and the ground troops had to slug ahead without air support.

As always, the engineers rose to the challenge. An airfield at Tacloban soon became one of the world's busiest. And flying off it in their twin-tailed Lightnings were Majors Richard Bong and Thomas McGuire. By December Bong had thirty-six planes to his credit, and McGuire had twenty-eight. General MacArthur gave Bong the Medal of Honor. Placing his hands on the stocky flier's shoulders, he said:

"Major Richard Ira Bong, who has ruled the air from New Guinea to the Philippines, I now induct you into the society of the bravest of the brave, the wearers of the Congressional Medal of Honor of the United States."

Majors Richard Bong (left) and Thomas McGuire.

Major Bong got two more planes to become America's ace of aces with forty kills. Tommy McGuire came close to equaling this feat. His score was thirty-eight before he was killed trying to save another pilot's life.

Supported from the air by Marine Corps squadrons, the American ground troops moved ahead. General Mac-Arthur's soldiers conquered Leyte soon after Christmas.

The General then turned to the vital northern island of Luzon. Here was the scene of the American defeat in 1942, and here was Manila, the beautiful capital of the Philippines. Here also was the scene of one of General MacArthur's most brilliant maneuvers. Before the battle, he said:

"With my Eighth Army off the southern coast of Luzon . . . I will threaten landings at . . . southern ports and draw the bulk of the Japanese into the south. This done, I will land the Sixth Army . . . on the exposed northern shore, thus cutting off the enemy's supplies from Japan. This will draw the enemy back to the north, leaving the Eighth Army to land against only weak opposition on the south coast. Both forces ashore, with but minor loss, will then close like a vise on the enemy . . . and destroy him."

This is exactly what happened during January of 1945. But once the Americans were ashore on both ends of Luzon, the fighting became fierce and bloody. The Japanese soldier, taught to believe himself invincible in the attack, was actually just the opposite. He was one of history's finest defensive fighters. Holed up in mountain strongpoints, the Japanese held out right to the end of the war. Their defense of Manila itself was particularly stubborn. Yank soldiers had to blast them out of the city, house by house. Terrible American artillery barrages knocked down beautiful old Spanish-style buildings. American tanks dueled with Japanese artillery in the rubble. Beautiful Manila was wrecked, and many civilians were killed and injured.

In the meantime, thousands of American prisoners of war had been liberated. Civilians, too, were freed of their cruel captors. It was discovered that tens of thousands had died. The horrible details of The Death March of American prisoners were made known. During three dreadful years, the Japanese had shown themselves as brutal and inhuman as the Nazis.

But none of those Americans who were set free had ever doubted that their countrymen would one day come to rescue them.

And they had.

31 | Germany Collapses

After the Allies had invaded France, Adolf Hitler told his generals: "My chance will come in the snows and fogs of winter." He did not explain this mysterious remark until, in the fall of 1944, he called a meeting at his Eagle's Nest in Bavaria.

Pale, his hands trembling, his left arm twitching, his leg dragging behind him as he walked—all the results of the attempted assassination—Hitler told his generals of his plan to smash the Allies with one stroke. A surprise attack of twenty-five divisions was to be launched through the Ardennes Forest into the center of the Allied line. It would be aimed mainly at the Americans, in a sector where the troops were thinly spread out. It would not fail.

Marshal von Rundstedt, who was to lead the operation, argued against it.

Hitler would not listen.

Under cover of darkness and the bad flying weather of winter, expert German divisions were moved into the thick woods of the Ardennes. Commando Otto Skorzeny, the man who had led the daring rescue of Mussolini, began training a special force of English-speaking Germans. They were issued American uniforms and taught American mannerisms. Their mission was to infiltrate the American rear and cause havoc.

On December 16, 1944, the Germans in the Ardennes laid down a shattering artillery barrage on the Americans. Then von Rundstedt's hordes attacked.

Unfortunately they hit green American troops and units exhausted by a bitter battle in the Huertgen Forest. Worse, the weather was so foul that Allied air power was useless.

The Germans broke through the American lines. They tore open a hole forty-five miles wide. Armored columns began racing for the River Meuse, where the Allies had huge stores of supplies. They drove a deep bulge into the Allied line. Because of it, this famous last-gasp German action has been called The Battle of the Bulge.

Early German successes did not upset General Eisenhower. He ordered reinforcements into the besieged town of Bastogne and sent General Patton charging up from the south to relieve the American garrison there.

Bastogne was the key to the entire Bulge. This little Belgian town was in the center of von Rundstedt's drive. His divisions were encircling it. If he could take it, the rear of his advancing troops would be safe. He would possess a fine road center. But the Americans in Bastogne fought bravely. They reddened the snowy hills with their blood, but they would not surrender.

December 22 the Germans sent two officers into Bastogne under a flag of truce. They told the Americans they were surrounded and under the muzzles of masses of heavy guns. They demanded the "honorable surrender of the encircled town." Brigadier General Anthony McAuliffe, in command at Bastogne, issued the famous one-word reply:

"Nuts!"

The Germans were mystified. "But what does it mean?" one of them asked. Whereupon an American colonel proceeded to explain the slang term in even less polite language. "And I can tell you something else," he added. "If you continue to attack, we will kill every German who tries to break into this city."

The Germans saluted. "We will kill many Americans," one of them said, but the colonel merely grinned and said: "On your way, Bud."

So General McAuliffe's gallant Americans continued to hold off the desperate Germans. Then the weather cleared and Allied planes were able to pound the enemy. Soon von Rundstedt found his own forces being squeezed on every side of the town. Patton's tanks entered Bastogne from the south, and Montgomery's divisions were slugging down from the north.

By mid-January of 1945 the Germans had withdrawn from the Bulge. Hitler's win-the-war offensive had ended in utter defeat. At the same time, the Russians launched their nonstop drive on Berlin. And the dreadful losses which the victorious Americans had inflicted on the Germans in the Bulge left the Wehrmacht with paper-thin defenses against the Russians in the east.

By the next month, the western Allies were also plunging into Germany.

The Battle of the Bulge

December 16, 1944, to January 16, 1945

US **1** *U.S. First Army*
US **3** *U.S. Third Army*

Route of the German attack
Direction of U.S. counterattack
Area of German penetration

Brigadier General Anthony McAuliffe, famous defender of Bastogne.

In February of 1945 the Allied line in the west ran straight down from the North Sea to the Mediterranean. General Ike had no less than seven armies ranged along this massive front.

In the north were the Canadian First, British Second, and United States Ninth armies under Field Marshal Montgomery. In the center were the United States First and Third armies under General Bradley. In the south were the United States Seventh and French First armies under Lieutenant General Jacob L. Devers.

They began battling up to the Rhine.

Not since Napoleonic times had this great broad water been crossed. The Germans always counted on their Rhine as one of the world's safest barriers. Besides, Hitler had reinforced it to the west with the Siegfried Line. The weather also favored the Germans. An early thaw made ribbons of mud of the roads, enmiring Allied armor. Still the advance struggled forward, and on February 21 the Allies reached the Rhine.

The Germans pulled back across the river.

During the next two days the Allies contented themselves with pouring ruin from the skies on the German rear. Planes of the Royal Air Force and the United States Eighth, Ninth, Twelfth and Fifteenth air forces flew 16,000 sorties and dropped 20,000 tons of explosives in western Germany. Still the Germans continued fortifying the Rhine barrier, blowing up every bridge in sight.

But they missed one.

Captain Willi Bratge had been ordered to blow up the Ludendorff Bridge at Remagen at exactly 4:00 P.M. on March 7, 1945. Even as German engineers fixed their charges to the bridge in the morning of that gray, drizzly day, they could hear American armor battling into the town. By half-past three in the afternoon, the onrushing Yanks had reached the bridge.

The Germans blew one weak charge. A few minutes later a stronger charge exploded.

There was another rumble and roar, and then an American lieutenant yelled:

"Look—she's still standing!"

She was, and to urgent cries of "Get going! Get going" the Americans began running over the bridge. Sergeant Alex Drabik was the first American to set foot on the east bank of the Rhine. Others joined him. By four o'clock there were one hundred Yanks clinging to this slim but precious foothold inside Germany's defensive barrier. The main charge of T.N.T. had failed to go off!

Behind them engineers worked furiously to repair the damaged bridge. Trucks and tanks began to cross. Within twenty-four hours there were eight thousand Americans across the Rhine. Then two more temporary bridges were built, one in less than thirty hours, an-

The bridge at Remagen, captured intact by the Americans.

other in less than forty.

The Germans struck back hard.

The Luftwaffe sent twenty-one of its new jet bombers to destroy the Remagen bridges. They failed. Eleven new V-2 rockets were fired at Remagen, and these also missed their target. All efforts to dislodge the American ground forces on the other side were hurled back.

Ten days after Sergeant Drabik pelted madly across the river, the Ludendorff Bridge, which one American general said was "worth its weight in gold," at last collapsed and fell into the river. But by then it was not needed. Working under fire, American engineers had thrown no less than sixty-two temporary bridges of all types across the "impassable" Rhine River.

All along that enormous front, now, seven Allied armies were surging across the Rhine. They went over by every means—amphibious trucks, landing craft, pontoon bridge, prefabricated bridge—and they drove deep into the heartland of collapsing Germany.

General Patton's freewheeling Third Army was out in front as usual. By April 23 Patton's armor had crossed the frontier of Czechoslovakia.

Two days later the onrushing Russians in the east and the rampaging Yanks in the west joined forces. They met at Torgau on the Elbe about seventy-five miles south of Berlin. Riflemen from both sides reached out to shake hands over what was, in effect, the prostrate body of the German nation.

And now the end was overtaking the very men who had set all this killing and destruction in motion.

On April 25, 1945, the Allied armies in Italy were driving toward Milan, the center of Mussolini's puppet government. Il Duce fled. He took with him his lady friend, Clara Petacci, and a hoard of gold. He put himself under German protection. But the Germans were also retreating and they could not care less about the "sawdust Caesar," as Mussolini was now called.

Three days later an Italian lieutenant colonel named Valerio found Mussolini and Miss Petacci in a farmhouse on Lake Como. Valerio strode inside Il Duce's room. Mussolini protested, but Valerio said, "I have come to free you." Then he and his men pushed Mussolini and Miss Petacci outside.

Il Duce became terrified.

"Let me go," he pleaded. "I will give you an empire!"

Valerio ignored his pleas and pushed them both into an automobile. The car stopped at a lonely spot along the road. Valerio stepped out.

"Get out quickly, both of you. Stand at the corner of that wall."

In terror they obeyed.

Valerio raised his pistol. "I execute the will of the Italian people," he said, and shot them both dead.

Their bodies were brought to Milan and hung on display in a public square. An infuriated Italian mob gathered to spit and kick at the body of the fallen tyrant. Then peace was restored and both bodies were buried in secret.

In Berlin, the end was also not long

The Third Army storms through the streets of a German city.

in coming.

American and British air power had made a gaunt and blackened skeleton of Hitler's capital city. Russian artillery pounded it from three sides. Deadly battles raged daily within the vast network of trenches and bunkers outside Berlin, and within its barricaded streets. At night, flames licked at the sky.

Below the ruined Reich Chancellery, in a maze of bunkers, Adolf Hitler refused to admit defeat.

He held daily conferences among his last-ditch followers. He issued orders to destroyed units or called for last-man defenses in areas that had long since fallen to the Allies. He pretended that he was still at the head of a vast and smooth-working war machine, instead of the broken remnant that reeled beneath the sledgehammer blows falling from east and west.

Then came the betrayals.

On April 22, 1945, Hitler received this communication from his old and trusted friend, Hermann Goering:

"My Fuehrer: In view of your decision to remain at your post in the fortress of Berlin, do you agree that I take over immediately the total leadership of the Reich . . . ?"

This was followed by Heinrich Himmler's attempts to negotiate a separate surrender with the Western Allies. The offer was coldly refused, but knowledge of it drove Hitler into an insane fury.

"Nothing now remains!" he screamed. "Nothing is spared me. No loyalty is kept, no honor observed! There is no bitterness, no betrayal that has not yet been heaped upon me."

On April 29, Hitler expelled Goering and Himmler from the Nazi party and named Admiral Doenitz as his successor. Then the tottering Fuehrer took a wife. In a lunatic ceremony within the narrow, airless rooms of his bunker, Hitler married Eva Braun, a blonde Bavarian woman who had been his devoted friend for many years. Next day he had his favorite dog, Blondi, destroyed. Then the Fuehrer shook hands with all his followers, including Dr. Joseph Goebbels, who had brought his wife and children to the bunker.

Above, Russian artillery shells were crashing into the Chancellery courtyard.

At 3:15 P.M., pale, trembling, Adolf Hitler walked to his room and shot himself through the mouth. Beside him lay the body of his new wife, who had taken poison.

Then Dr. Goebbels poisoned his six little children, and stood beside his wife while Nazi guards carefully shot them through the head.

Thus came the horrible end of the

Field Marshal Wilhelm Keitel signs the ratified surrender terms for the German army at Russian headquarters in Berlin.

men who had unleashed the Nazi horror on the world. Other leading Nazis who did not kill themselves as Himmler did later, were rounded up and brought to trial as war criminals. Eleven of them, led by Goering, were sentenced to be hanged, although Goering dodged the hangman by swallowing poison.

And one week after Hitler put the pistol in his mouth, Admiral Doenitz surrendered Germany to the Allies.

Surrender terms were signed at General Eisenhower's headquarters in a red-brick schoolhouse at Reims, France, on May 7, 1945. It was ratified two days later at the Russian headquarters in Berlin.

The Nazi beast was dead, and now there remained only the task of finishing off Japan.

32 | The Flag Flies at Iwo

While General MacArthur's men were liberating the Philippines, Admiral Nimitz resumed his drive on Tokyo.

He had two objectives: Iwo Jima and Okinawa. Iwo was to be the first. This was because "Sulphur Island," as the Japanese called it, was only 760 miles south of Tokyo. It would serve as an emergency landing point for the big B-29 bombers flying from Marianas bases to Japan. Many B-29s were lost, with their crews, on the return flight.

Iwo was a tiny cinder clog of an island, only four and a half miles long, and two and a half miles wide. From the air it looked like a lopsided black pork chop. At its southern tip was a squat volcano named Mount Suribachi.

But Iwo was fortified beyond all imagination. Where Peleliu had had 500 caves, Iwo had 1,500 of them. Where Tarawa had had hundreds of thick-walled pillboxes, Iwo had twice as many of them—and most of them below ground. All of the 21,000 men defending Iwo had been told to fight to the death. They recited their Courageous Battle Vow, which went, in part:

We shall grasp bombs, charge the
    enemy tanks and destroy them.
We shall infiltrate into the midst of
    the enemy and annihilate them.
With every salvo we will, without
    fail, kill the enemy.
Each man will make it his duty to
    kill ten of the enemy before

dying.

These men were ordered to lie low during American air and sea bombardments. They were not to return fire and risk giving away their concealed positions. It was the Japanese commander's plan to allow the Americans one hour in which to get their troops ashore. Then all the terrific fire power of Iwo's hidden guns would fall upon them and destroy them.

On February 19, 1945, two of Admiral Nimitz's three divisions of Marines stormed Iwo's terraced beaches. In an hour all the assault battalions were landed and bucking across the island.

Then the Japanese opened up.

Shells shrieked and crashed among the Marines. Harmless-looking hummocks spat automatic fire. The very beaches began to erupt with exploding land mines.

The enemy fire was hardest on the reserve troops coming in after the assault units. They could not get below ground because it was impossible to dig a foxhole in Iwo's volcanic ash. Most vehicles could not roll in the cinders, either, and the amtracs and tanks were unable to climb the beach terraces. Beneath one of the terraces, a young officer cried:

"If you want to win this war let's get up there!"

He swung his arm at the top of the terrace, and fell dead. But his men

The Marines land at Iwo. (Mount Suribachi shows dimly in the background.)

clambered over his body and began crawling inland.

Even so, the Japanese gunners were taking a terrible toll among the brave American Marines. It appeared that the Japanese commander would carry out his plan. Iwo's landing beaches were a horrifying battleground, a litter of dead and wounded, of wrecked and burning vehicles. Out in the water, boats were burning and sinking and Marine amphibious tanks were wallowing in the swells while dueling Japanese pillboxes.

However, one hour had been enough for the Marines to gain their foothold. They held it and gradually expanded it. By nightfall, they were there to stay.

In the morning, big Colonel Harry ("Harry the Horse") Liversedge led his Marine regiment to the south in the assault on Mount Suribachi.

This was Iwo's highest ground. Atop Suribachi, the Japanese not only could watch every Marine move and report it to the commander in the north; they could direct scorching artillery fire on the Americans.

That first day of attack, the Marines gained only two hundred yards. At night, the Japanese marked the American lines with flares. From the north a whistling rain of shells fell on the Marines.

In the morning, supported by aircraft, naval and land artillery, and massed tanks and amtracs, the Marines drove to the volcano's base.

"At dawn," said Harry the Horse, "we start climbing."

That third day the Marines went up Suribachi in a magnificent fighting climb. They flushed the enemy out of caves with flame throwers or drove them over cliffs. They reached the top at half-past ten in the morning and raised a flag above it. But it was a tiny flag and no one could see it. Another, larger flag was raised in its place. An Associated Press photographer named Joe Rosenthal took a picture as six men—one of them a

Navy corpsman—struggled to get Old Glory into place.

That picture became the most famous of the war. Of the brave men who were in it, three were later killed and one was wounded.

Caught and flung by the strong winds whipping Suribachi's crest, the Stars and Stripes inspired those grimy, doughty Marines below who were even then slowly slugging north.

It was like attacking into a deadly Chinese box. The fall of one defensive Japanese position would unmask another stronger one. The noise of whizzing bullets was constant. Men scarcely dared take a step for fear of thousands of "kettle mines" planted in the cinders.

A third Marine division entered the battle, and still the Japanese defenses held.

To the rear, in the shadow of Suribachi, an emergency landing field was being built. On March 4, a B-29 running low on gasoline made a successful landing there. Before the war ended, 2,251 Superforts with 24,761 crewmen were saved by emergency landings on Iwo Jima.

Three days after the first Superfort landed, the Marines broke through the enemy center in a daring night attack. In darkness, while a whistling wind hurled cold rain in their faces, the Americans stole up on a Japanese strongpoint. They came upon the enemy asleep in their trenches and wiped them out.

With daylight, a terrible battle began raging. It went on for days. But the Marines gradually widened the hole punched in the enemy's center. Tanks and yelling riflemen began pouring through the gap. The enemy was herded into a pocket on the end of the island.

One night a thousand of them tied explosives around their waists and tried to force a way to the airfield where they intended to wreck equipment. Almost all of these "human bombs" were killed, many of them blowing up when struck by bullets.

But Iwo—the bloodiest and most renowned battle in the history of the Marines—never came to a sudden, stirring end. It was shot for shot, grenade for grenade from beginning to end, until, on March 26, the Stars and Stripes waved over all of the island.

On the same day, the Americans began assaulting the offshore islands west of Okinawa.

Old Glory flies on Mount Suribachi.

33 | Okinawa: The Last Battle

Okinawa lay about 350 miles south of Japan. Almost seventy miles long, it was big enough to provide a "staging area" for the great masses of troops and equipment against the day when Japan herself would be invaded. Okinawa was also within easy range of the new weapon with which Japan hoped to stave off defeat.

This was the *Kamikaze.*

Kamikaze means "divine wind." It refers to an event immortal in Japanese history. In 1570 an emperor of China gathered a great fleet to invade Nippon. But a "divine wind" in the shape of a typhoon sprang up to scatter the Chinese fleet.

In 1945, young suicide pilots pledged that they would dive their bomb-laden

General Simon B. Buckner (left), commanding general of the Tenth Army, and Marine General Roy S. Geiger.

aircraft into enemy ships. They were called Kamikazes. The first of them had appeared off the Philippines in October of 1944. At Iwo Jima, a Kamikaze crashed and sank the escort carrier *Bismarck Sea* and badly damaged big *Saratoga* and others.

Thousands of them were ready by April 1, 1945, the date of the Okinawa invasion. Because of this, Lieutenant General Mitsuru Ushijima had been ordered to fight a defensive battle. His 32nd Army was to dig in and delay the Americans so that the supporting ships would be exposed to Kamikaze attack for as long as possible.

There were 1,300 American ships in this great invasion fleet. Although this was not as many as the 2,727 Allied vessels which crossed the Channel on D-Day, these were all big ships and many of them were sailing as far as 7,200 miles to the battle.

Okinawa was to be the greatest amphibious assault of all time, even bigger than D-Day. There were 183,000 men in the attack force alone, four Army and three Marine divisions. They made up the Tenth Army, commanded by Lieutenant General Simon Bolivar Buckner, Jr., the "Old Man of the Mountain." Son of the famous Confederate general of the same name, Buckner was a big, ruddy-faced, white-haired man.

General Buckner was highly pleased with the first reports on L-Day, or

"Love-Day" as the troops called it.

There was almost no opposition.

Two Marine divisions on the left, two Army divisions on the right had seized a beachhead eight miles wide on Okinawa's western coast. Supplies and additional thousands of exultant troops began pouring ashore. The vanguards swept inland, easily capturing two airfields the first day. In three days the island was cut in two.

Then the Marines wheeled left to clean out the fortified mountains of the north, and the soldiers turned right to batter their way south.

It was in the south that General Ushijima had built his formidable cross-island defense. But the Americans had not quite uncovered its true strength before men near the coasts could hear ships' bull horns blaring:

"Attention! Attention! All hands! President Roosevelt is dead. Repeat, our Commander in Chief, President Roosevelt, is dead."

Swiftly the news reached men out of earshot. Like their comrades around the world and their countrymen at home, they were stunned. Many of them cried. President Roosevelt had been beloved.

Soon they heard the details. Shortly after noon on April 12, 1945, the President was sitting for a portrait at the Little White House in Warm Springs, Georgia. Suddenly he said: "I have a terrific headache." These were his last words. He lost consciousness and died of a cerebral hemorrhage.

Vice President Harry S. Truman succeeded Mr. Roosevelt in the White House.

A group of machine gunners and BAR men fire at Japanese positions on Okinawa.

On Okinawa, the jubilant Japanese pretended that Mr. Roosevelt had died upon hearing news of the "destruction" of the American fleet around Okinawa. They printed propaganda leaflets to this effect.

It was false, of course, although it was certainly true that the Kamikaze had by then become the American sailor's scourge.

Day after day the Japanese suiciders pressed home their attacks. They struck generally at destroyers of the picket line, often in the mistaken belief that they were diving on cruisers and battleships.

They dived suddenly out of the blue. Even if they were hit, it often made no difference: momentum carried the flaming Kamikaze unerringly to its target.

181

Swift and searing were the suffering and destruction caused by the Kamikaze. And the strain placed upon the American seamen was almost beyond endurance.

They had to keep their ships "buttoned up" at all times. They were at battle stations twenty-four hours on end. They sometimes fought off hundreds of screaming suiciders in desperate battles lasting for hours. Sailors below decks moved like wooden men, so thorough was their exhaustion and loss of energy from the heat. In the face of all this, the American bluejackets fought on, always assisted by the brave, tireless aviators of all services who flew from carrier decks or off Okinawa airfields to help hurl back the Kamikaze threat.

On land, meanwhile, General Buckner employed five divisions abreast to punch through Ushijima's defenses.

Much of the fighting on Okinawa resembled the dogged slugging matches fought on Iwo Jima. But where the loose shifting volcanic ash had been the main drawback of Iwo's terrain, Okinawa's most miserable feature was its mud. Some days the leaky skies above this long, irregular island were capable of pouring out ten inches of rain. The rains made a mud that was everywhere. It got inside a man's ears, under his nails, inside his leggings, or was squeezed—coarse and cold—between his toes. There was mud inside a man's weapon, in his food, within his mouth. If a man was unfortunate enough to be hit in the rain, there would be mud in his wound.

Mud made a mockery of attempts to build roads, and made it next to impossible to supply these slowly advancing Americans with food.

Nevertheless, the attack continued to go forward: Army on the left, Marines on the right. Almost to the end, American warships stood off the seaward flanks to pound the enemy, and American aircraft swooped down on him from the skies.

On May 29 the American flag waved over Shuri Castle, ancient capital of the island and General Ushijima's former headquarters.

On June 18 victory was in sight. General Buckner visited the front to observe one of the final attacks. He stood on Mezado Ridge, watching intently. "Things are going so well here," he said, "I think I'll move on to another unit."

Five Japanese shells shrieked and crashed on Mezado Ridge.

General Buckner fell, a shard of flying coral in his chest. He died ten minutes later, comforted in the knowledge that his Tenth Army was winning the battle.

Lieutenant General Roy Geiger of the Marines took his place. General Geiger had been at Guadalcanal in the beginning of the American counteroffensive. Now he was to be in command at the end on Okinawa.

Victory came three days later, when an American patrol reached Ara Point to gaze down upon the mingling waters of the Pacific Ocean and the East China Sea. That night General Ushijima committed suicide.

After eighty-three days of some of the bitterest fighting of the war Okinawa was in American hands.

The End of a Titanic Conflict | 34

America's leaders had not expected Okinawa to be the last battle.

It was considered merely the prelude to the titanic struggle for Japan itself. This was scheduled to begin in November of 1945.

Ships and men and arms from the European Theater were already speeding to the Pacific to join that million-man invasion.

But Japan was already beaten by the time Okinawa fell. The military fanatics still refused to believe it, but the fall of Okinawa gave the Japanese "peace party" the opportunity to make them face some facts.

First of all, Japan had no navy left, and she had lost her merchant fleet. The American submarines—unsung heroes of World War Two—had achieved what Admiral Doenitz and his U-boats had not been able to accomplish against England. By the summer of 1945, they had cut all lifelines to Japan. They were prowling off the enemy coast and sinking inter-island ferries in the inland sea itself. In all, American submarines sank sixty per cent of the 2,117 Japanese merchant vessels lost in World War Two, as well as 201 of the Japanese warships sent to the bottom.

Added to this was the terrible rain of destruction falling upon the home islands. Giant B-29s had been striking at Japanese cities in 300-plane raids. On March 9 the Superforts came down to

6,000 feet over Tokyo to drop fire bombs that burned up a quarter of a million homes, made a million people homeless and killed 83,793 persons. This stands as the most lethal air raid in all history.

And a huge American bombardment fleet had been sailing right up to the shores of Nippon to bomb and shell factories and steel plants. In cruising formation this vast armada covered an area forty miles long and nine miles wide. When commanded by Admiral Halsey it was called the Third Fleet; when led by Admiral Spruance it was the Fifth Fleet.

Finally, the loss of hundreds of Japanese planes at Okinawa had destroyed the Japanese Air Force.

Unable to wage war, her people at the point of starvation, Japan was in no position to prolong the struggle. Yet her militarists fought all talk of peace. Members of Baron Suzuki's "peace party" did not press them, fearing assassination.

Then came August 6, 1945. A huge silvery Superfort named *Enola Gay* thundered aloft from Tinian in the Marianas. It flew over Hiroshima and dropped the world's first atomic bomb. In that single flash of pure light and ensuing fireball, an entire city was destroyed and 78,000 people lost their lives.

Still the militarists refused to surrender.

On August 8, Russia declared war on

183

Japan. Next day the world's second atomic bomb was dropped on Nagasaki.

The following day President Truman called upon the Japanese to give up.

On August 14 a momentous meeting of Japan's "elder statesmen" was held in the presence of Emperor Hirohito. Once again the "war party" argued against surrender. The meeting came to a deadlock. The deadlock was broken by Hirohito, whose word was law though he rarely spoke. The Emperor insisted on surrender.

"We demand that you will agree to it," he said. "We see only one way left for Japan to save herself. That is the reason we have made this determination to endure the unendurable and suffer the insufferable."

On that day—August 14, 1945—Japan gave up.

Her surrender was received by General Douglas MacArthur in formal ceremonies aboard mighty U.S.S. *Missouri* in Tokyo Bay on September 2, 1945.

World War II had raged for six years and a day. It had caused ruin and torment unrivaled in the annals of human suffering. It had ended with America and Russia all-powerful on earth, confronting each other as old friends and new enemies. It had ushered in the dreadful era of nuclear warfare. It had brought death to thirty million human beings, soldiers and civilians alike, men, women, and children.

It had done all this, and now the greatest war in history was over.

General of the Army Douglas MacArthur signs the Japanese surrender document. At left are General Jonathan Wainwright, U.S. Army, and General A. E. Percival, British Army, both freed from Japanese captivity by Allied victory.

Japanese representatives arrive aboard the USS Missouri *to participate in formal surrender ceremonies.*

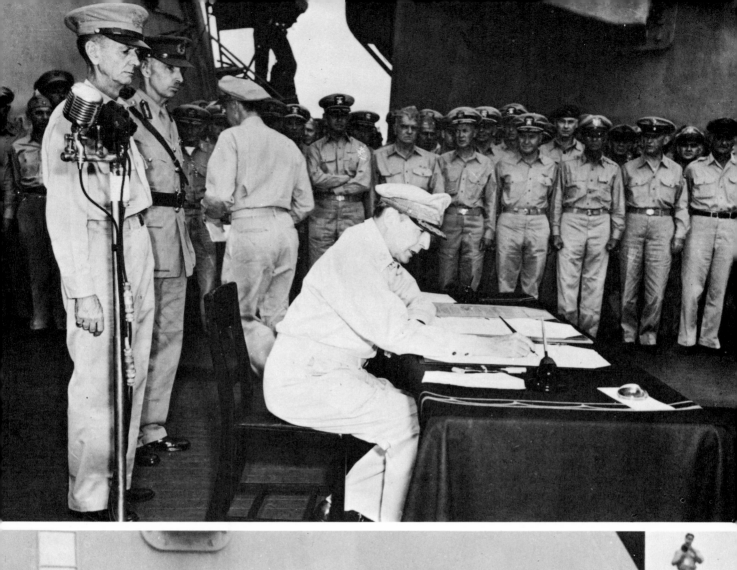

A Chronological Listing
of Selected Highlights

1939

Sept.   1   Germany army invades Poland.

3   Great Britain, France declare war on Germany. British liner *Athenia* torpedoed by German U-boat. Winston Churchill becomes Britain's First Lord of the Admiralty.

Sept.   17   Russia invades eastern Poland.

27   Poland surrenders to Germany.

Nov.   30   Russia invades Finland.

Dec.   17   German pocket battleship *Graf Spee* scuttled off Montevideo. Finns rout Russians in two-day battle.

1940

March   12   Finnish-Russian war ends in Russia's favor.

April   9   Germany invades Denmark and Norway. Denmark capitulates. Norway fights.

May   10   Germany invades Holland, Belgium, and Luxembourg. Winston Churchill replaces Neville Chamberlain as prime minister of Britain.

15   Holland surrenders; Germans drive south through Belgium.

26   British order the evacuation of Dunkirk.

28   Belgian army surrenders to Germans.

June   8   British withdraw from Norway.

10   Italy declares war on France and Great Britain.

June   22   French sign armistice dictated by Germans; fighting ends in France.

July   10   Battle of Britain begins.

Sept.   7   The London Blitz starts.

14   Italians drive into Egypt from Libya.

27   Japan joins the Rome-Berlin Axis.

Oct.   28   Italy invades Greece.

Nov.   19   Greeks rout Italians and pursue them into Albania.

20   Hungary joins the Axis powers.

23   Rumania joins the Axis powers.

Dec.   15   Italian troops driven out of Egypt by British Commonwealth forces; seesaw battle for North Africa begins.

1941

March   1   Bulgaria joins the Axis.

11   President Roosevelt signs Lend-Lease Bill passed by Congress.

25   Yugoslav government joins Axis, but two days later a group of army officers overthrow government and defy Germany.

April   3   German mechanized forces join Italians in launching a new offensive in North Africa.

6   Germans move against Yugoslav rebels, attack Greece.

18   Yugloslav army surrenders; guerrilla warfare continues.

27   Athens falls to Germany.

May   20   Germany attacks Crete with airborne troops.

27   British planes sink *Bismarck*.

June   1   Britain announces surrender of Crete.

22   Germany invades Russia.

Oct.   11   Hideki Tojo is named premier of Japan.

14   Germans drive to within 60 miles of Moscow.

Dec.   7   Japanese bomb Pearl Harbor.

8   United States declares war on Japan; Britain follows. Japan invades Thailand.

9   Japanese land in Malaya.

10   First Japanese landings on Luzon in the Philippines.

11   Germany and Italy declare war on the United States.

22   Major Japanese invasion of the Philippines.

23   Wake Island falls to Japan.

1942

Jan. 2 Japanese occupy Manila; General MacArthur's troops fall back to Bataan.

14 German submarines begin torpedoing U. S. tankers off East Coast.

Feb. 15 Singapore surrenders.

27 Allied fleet battered by Japanese in Battle of the Java Sea.

March 7 Japanese enter Rangoon, Burma.

9 Java falls to Japanese, concluding Netherlands East Indies campaign.

31 German-Italian force opens offensive in Libya.

April 9 Bataan falls to Japan; Americans retreat to Corregidor.

18 Tokyo bombed by U. S. Army planes taking off from Navy carrier *Hornet*.

May 4-8 Battle of the Coral Sea; Japanese invasion fleet turned back from Port Moresby, New Guinea.

6 Corregidor falls.

12 Germany renews Russian offensive.

27 Germans drive back British in Libya.

June 4-6 Battle of Midway.

25 Axis forces penetrate 50 miles into Egypt.

July 3 Sevastopol, great Russian bastion on Black Sea, falls to German and Rumanian forces.

28 Japanese launch overland drive on Port Moresby from Buna in New Guinea.

Aug. 7 U. S. Marines land on Guadalcanal, Tulagi in Solomon Islands.

8-9 Battle of Savo Island.

Sept. 14 Germans launch massive attack on Stalingrad.

Oct. 24 British open offensive at El Alamein in Egypt.

Nov. 8 British and American troops begin landings in North Africa.

12-15 Naval Battle of Guadalcanal ends with American victory over Japanese.

12 British retake Tobruk.

Dec. 3 Russians break through German lines after raising siege of Stalingrad.

1943

Jan. 5 Germany begins withdrawal from entire Stalingrad area.

14 President Roosevelt confers with Churchill at Casablanca, makes demand for "unconditional surrender."

18 Russia announces that the 17-month siege of Leningrad has been raised.

22 United States-Australian force recaptures Buna from Japanese.

Feb. 9 Japanese evacuate Guadalcanal.

March 2-4 Allied land-based planes inflict decisive defeat on Japanese in Battle of the Bismarck Sea.

May 7 Americans take Bizerte in Tunisia; British enter Tunis.

July 10 Allies invade Sicily.

Aug. 1 Americans bomb Ploesti oil fields in Rumania.

Sept. 3 British land in Italy; Italian government signs secret armistice.

9 Allies invade Italy in force.

11 Americans capture Salamaua in New Guinea.

16 Japanese base at Lae in New Guinea falls.

Oct. 1 American Fifth Army captures Naples.

2 Australians retake Finschhafen in New Guinea.

Nov. 1 Americans land on Bougainville in northern Solomons.

20 Americans land on Tarawa and Makin in the Gilberts.

Dec. 15 Americans land on Arawe in New Britain.

26 Americans assault Japanese on Cape Gloucester in New Britain.

1944

Jan. 22 Allied troops land on Italy's west coast as Anzio campaign begins.

Feb. 1 Americans make landings on Kwajalein Atoll.

Feb. 15 Bombers leave historic Monte Cassino Abbey in ruins.

17 Americans assault Eniwetok Atoll.

March 8 Russians drive to within 80 miles of Rumania.

May 10 Russians recapture Sevastopol.

June 4 Allies enter Rome.

6 Invasion of France begun under General Eisenhower.

15 Americans land on Saipan.

19 Japanese navy badly beaten by the United States in Battle of the Philippine Sea.

July 12 Germany's eastern border menaced by Russians.

21 Americans land on Guam.

24 Americans assault Tinian.

25 Americans break through German lines in Normandy.

30 General MacArthur's New Guinea drive ends on Sansapor Point.

Aug. 15 Allies invade southern France.

24 Rumania surrenders and joins the Allies.

Aug. 25 German commandant surrenders Paris; General de Gaulle enters city.

Sept. 4 Allies take Brussels and Antwerp in Belgium, cross Dutch border.

12 Americans cross German border.

15 Americans land on Peleliu.

24 Russians advance into Czechoslovakia, threaten Hungary.

Oct. 2 Americans begin new attacks on Siegfried Line.

20 Americans return to the Philippines with landings on Leyte. Russians cross German border.

23-26 U. S. Navy destroys remnant of Japanese navy in Battle of Leyte Gulf.

Dec. 16 German counteroffensive opens Battle of the Bulge.

30 Germans finally stopped; Bulge becomes American victory.

1945

Jan. 9 Americans invade Luzon in northern Philippines.

22 Russians within ten miles of Oder River, sign armistice with Hungary.

Feb. 5 Americans enter Manila.

7 Roosevelt, Churchill, and Stalin meet at Yalta.

19 Americans land on Iwo Jima.

March 7 Americans take Remagen Bridge in Germany and cross the Rhine.

April 1 Americans land on Okinawa.

11 Americans within 90 miles of Berlin; Russians enter Vienna.

12 President Roosevelt dies.

28 Mussolini executed by Italian partisans.

May 1 Hitler kills himself in Berlin.

7 Germany surrenders unconditionally.

June 17 President Truman, Churchill, and Stalin meet at Potsdam.

22 Okinawa, last ground battle of the war, ends in victory for Americans.

July 15 U. S. Navy begins surface bombardment of Japan.

29 Japan rejects surrender ultimatum.

Aug. 6 First atomic bomb in history dropped on Hiroshima.

9 Second atomic bomb dropped on Nagasaki.

14 Japan accepts surrender terms.

Sept. 2 Japanese sign surrender in Tokyo Bay and the war ends.

Index

189